Noel!

Curriculum Resources for Christmas

Key stage 1

Redvers Brandling

Nash Pollock
Publishing

© Redvers Brandling 1998

First published 1998 by
Nash Pollock Publishing
32 Warwick Street
Oxford OX4 1SX

10 9 8 7 6 5 4 3 2 1

Orders to:
York Publishing Services
64 Hallfield Road
Layerthorpe
York
YO3 7XQ

The author's moral right is asserted.

A catalogue record of this book is available from the British Library

ISBN 1 898255 20 2

Typeset in 11 on 14pt Melior by Black Dog Design, Buckingham
Illustrations by Trevor Mason and Clare Mattey
Printed in Great Britain by Redwood Books Ltd

Contents

(33 activity sheets have been prepared for use with this book. For ease of reference the contents list notes the number of worksheets which are associated with each chapter.

Acknowledgements

I am as always grateful to former staff and children of Dewhurst St Mary School, Cheshunt. For so many years they were a receptive audience for Christmas ideas, and a source of both inspiration and information with their own presentations.

I am grateful to Elizabeth Bywaters for letting me use her story 'Can you Help Father Christmas?' 'The Holly Tree's Story' and the idea for the 'Number Game' activity sheet first appeared in *Christmas is Coming*. Some of the material contained in the 'ABC of the Season' was used in *Christmas in the Primary School* (Ward Lock Educational). It has been greatly extended here.

The 'Illuminated boxes' theme is a development of an idea used in *Science Topics for Infants* (Blackwell). Two of the 'investigation games' are also derived from ideas used in this book.

The School Curriculum and Assessment Authority's *Model Syllabuses for Religious Education* remains a valuable source for multi-cultural reference. It can be recommended to all teachers.

If he has unwittingly caused any infringement of copyright in this book the author apologises and will correct the omission in future editions if notified.

Introduction

Christmas for young children is synonymous with joy and delight, and any book related to the season must complement these feelings. At the same time, as Denys Thompson said, teachers should be aware of rescuing 'the truths of Christmas from the commercial jungle'.

The modern teacher must also marry these two aims to a third – that of fulfilling National Curriculum criteria with the enormous amount of work which is associated with the season in infant schools.

This book seeks to offer practical help in each of these three areas. The chapter headings indicate the various approaches which can all be used for long term planning and detailed preparation. These features are supported by 33 children's activity sheets which are directly related to the work and ideas in the book.

Throughout the book there are reminders of when and where specific activity sheets can be used most effectively. Teachers of Key Stage 1 children need no reminders of course that their 'personal touch' when explaining and using such material is enormously advantageous.

For very many years I have found the vitality, enthusiasm, resourcefulness – and durability(!) of infant teachers an inspiring combination. This is particularly so at Christmas, and I hope this book will be another useful resource to add to their Christmas shelf.

An ABC of the Christmas Season

(Activity sheets 1 and 2)

One of the most admirable qualities of so many Key Stage 1 teachers is their ability to 'translate' often complex material into language understood by their charges. This is a huge asset because, like their Key Stage 2 counterparts, young children expect their teachers to be walking encyclopaedias!

This section is therefore basically one of information and reference for busy teachers. Christmas abounds in customs, events, associations and 'key words', and over the next few pages some details of these have been arranged in alphabetical order.

There are two activity sheets associated with this chapter. The answers for them are as follows:

Sheet 1

1 Jesus was born in a stable.

2 The stable was in a town called Bethlehem.

3 Jesus' mother was called Mary.

4 The three Kings followed a star in the sky.

5 This is called a candle.

6 We get presents at Christmas.

7 These children are singing carols.

8 This man looks after sheep. He is called a shepherd.

9 At Christmas we pull crackers.

10 At Christmas we hear bells ringing.

Sheet 2

1 Donkey (or Ass).

2 Shepherds.

3 They followed a star.

4 Gold or Frankincense or Myrrh.

7 25th December.

Advent

One of the dictionary's more prosaic descriptions of Advent is: 'an ecclesiastical division of the year embracing the four weeks before Christmas' (Gresham's *Comprehensive English Dictionary*). This description fails to reflect the astute thinking of the early rulers of the church who set about establishing the calendar time when Christmas would be celebrated. Recognising the fact that all momentous events are emphasised be a period of preparation and 'build up,' they determined Advent as the period leading up to Christmas. It reached its peak on Christmas Eve – a designated time of vigil.

Ass

The ass is a very familiar aspect of Nativity scenes, particularly those of Renaissance paintings. It symbolises the humblest of creatures being present when Jesus was born. ('The ox knoweth its owner, and the ass its master's crib.' Isiah 1:3)

Baboushka

One of the great legends of Christmas centres on Baboushka, an old Russian woman, known for her kindness and her ability to make wonderful black bread.

One morning she had a call from three important-looking men. They were in fact the Magi, on their journey to find the new-born king. They asked the old woman if they could rest awhile, and while doing so they told her about following the star and the special birth.

She asked if she might join them on the journey and take a humble present of black bread to the new-born King. They agreed but said she must accompany them immediately.

But Baboushka said she must tidy her cottage first. The kings left, and when Baboushka was ready to go it was dawn and the guiding star had disappeared. She followed the footsteps of the kings in the snow but eventually these faded too.

After that Baboushka travelled for weeks, never finding anybody who had seen the kings. Finally she met people who had heard of the special birth and at last she was guided to the stable. Jesus, Mary and Joseph were long gone but in the corner she saw the crib. Going to it she laid her present of black bread on the spot where Jesus had lain. Then the old exhausted woman lay down and died in the stable.

Her memory lives on in modern Russia. Children often find a piece of black bread amongst their Christmas presents – a sign that Baboushka has visited their home on her greater journeys. *Come and Praise* Vol. 2 contains a very attractive carol entitled 'Baboushka'.)

Bee

Honey is a symbol of Christ and the bee, as a producer of it, often symbolises Mary. Ancient legends suggest the bee never sleeps so it has also come to represent Christian vigilance.

Bells

The ringing of Church bells is particularly associated with Christmas, and the 'ringing in' of the season. At the parish church in Dewsbury in Yorkshire an old tradition has it that bells are tolled for every year that has passed since Jesus was born. This practice has been taking place for hundreds of years.

Bethlehem

Bethlehem in Judea, when Jesus was born, was a small town set amidst hills and olive groves. It was known as the City of David because it was here, centuries before, that David was born.

Another name for Bethlehem was 'the house of bread', because the district around the town was known as Ephrathah, meaning 'fruitful'.

The stable where Jesus was born was probably a cave in the hills around the town. These caves were used for storage and the housing of cattle.

Birthdays

Children born on 25 December (zodiac sign Capricorn) will no doubt be pleased to know that traditionally those born on this date combine qualities of determination and trustworthiness.

Boar's Head

It was in the 4th Century that the Church fixed 25 December as the date of Christ's birth. From then on banquets took place on Christmas Day and the main early dishes were a boar's head and a roasted peacock in which the feathers were still displayed. Turkeys did not arrive from America until the middle of the 16th Century.

Camel

The camel was looked upon as not only a means of transport and a beast of burden, but also as a sign of dignity with royal associations. As such it features in many depictions of the Three Wise Men, their journey, and their visit to Bethlehem.

Candles

Practically providing light, and also being symbolic of it, candles were 'an image of the starry heaven from which Christ would come'. Their use on Christmas trees was supposedly initiated by Martin Luther. The candle is also a symbol of hope.

Cards

Christmas cards, and examples of them, provide enough material for a book to themselves! For children they provide an endless fascination and many were specifically designed to please early recipients.

In the 1840s Henry Cole (later Sir Henry Cole, Director of the Victoria and Albert Museum) decided that, rather than send letters of good wishes to all his friends at Christmas time, he would send them cards. He got an actor friend, John Calcott Horsley, to design a card and the first Christmas card was sent in 1843.

There the fashion started. Early cards tended to feature hand-painted birds and flowers, supplemented by lacy surrounds and a Christmas message. In 1867 a 'frosty, wintry' look (obtained by blowing fine glass on them) was introduced to cards by the firm of Thierry, and from then on development was spectacular. Children in particular were delighted by cards from which theatrical scenes sprang up when tabs were pulled, flowers bloomed and windows opened. Other devices included the envelopes as part of the scene which opened up.

Through the Victorian era other common themes for Christmas cards were summer scenes, more wintry scenes, eventually depictions of the Nativity, soldiers, and in the 1890s the first comic ideas.

By the end of the 19th Century about 200,000 different designs had been devised.

Cat

An old legend which interests children claims that at the time Jesus was born a cat, which was also in the stable, gave birth to a litter of kittens.

Census

Palestine had become a small part of the Roman Empire in 63 BC. At the time Mary was about to have her baby, the Roman Emperor, Caesar

Augustus, wanted to know how many people lived in this part of the Empire so he could make sure they all paid taxes.

He thus determined that every man should return to the town where he was born and register in a taxation census. Thus Joseph, at a critical time in his family life, had to make the difficult journey from Nazareth to Bethlehem, the town of his birth.

Christingle

Some of the children may have been to a Christingle service, as they are increasing in popularity. At such a service each child receives a 'Christingle' – an orange which symbolises the world, surmounted by a candle which represents the Light of the World. Four cocktail sticks, each piercing a side of the orange and decorated with nuts and raisins, represent the seasons and the fruits of the earth. A red band tied round the centre of the orange is the final attachment and symbolises the blood of Christ, shed for the world.

When the candles on the Christingles are lit then carols of celebration are sung. Originally the tradition was one founded by the Moravian Church and the service was always held on Christmas Eve.

Coins

The old tradition of there being hidden coins in the Christmas pudding stemmed from the days when every member of the family took a turn at stirring the pudding. During this ritual it was thought that evil spirits could be warded off by introducing silver to the mixture – hence the addition of old silver threepenny pieces.

Colours

The significance of colours with regard to Christmas is apparent in several ways. In paintings of Mary holding the Christ Child she wears a blue mantle, symbolising heavenly love.

Green is the colour of the Epiphany and the coming of the Magi; purple is the colour of Advent, a time of preparation; white is a feature of Christmas services.

Crackers

Tom Smith is the name to be associated with crackers. A London confectioner, he decided that his packages of sweets and toys would have much greater attraction at Christmas if they could be pulled apart with a bang and then revealed what was inside. He started work on this idea in 1850; two years later the first crackers appeared and Tom Smith's prosperity was assured.

Eve

Christmas Eve is the time of midnight services and the blessing of the crib. The first Festival of Nine Lessons and Carols at King's College, Cambridge took place in 1918.

The famous 'truce' of the First World War took place on Christmas Eve 1914. Ignoring orders of their superiors ordinary soldiers of the English and German armies left their trenches to exchange presents, sing carols and play football. A British officer wrote at the time: 'all this talk of hate, all this fury at each other that has raged since the beginning of the war, quelled and stayed by the magic of Christmas'.

Fir

The fir tree is the symbol of patience.

Francis

St Francis of Assisi, patron saint of animals, is probably already known to the children. (Francis and the wolf of Gubbio is a very well known story.)

It was his re-creation of the manger scene in the 12th century, however, which started the tradition of nativity scenes so common at Christmas. Francis worked to establish the essential humility of the original birth scene and his re-creation was in a wood near Greccio in Italy. People from all around came to worship at this site.

Frankincense

One of the gifts of the Magi, Frankincense was made from rare natural oils and was thus very valuable. It symbolised divinity.

Gold

Another gift from the Magi, gold has always been highly prized. As the Magi were men of great wisdom who could see into the future their gift of gold was a symbol of royalty for the Christ Child.

Holly

Holly was incorporated into Christmas celebrations via the Roman Festival of Saturnalia. At this time the exchanging of evergreen sprigs of it symbolised friendship which would last forever. It was also considered 'sacred' in that it bore fruit in winter.

There are several appealing Christmas legends about the holly tree, and one can be found in the 'Prose and Poems' section of this book.

Ivy

Carols sing of 'the holly and the ivy' and the latter, being forever green, is a symbol of eternal life, and also attachment and everlasting affection.

Journeys

Nazareth, the home of Joseph and Mary, was a small town not far from the Sea of Galilee. To make the journey to Bethlehem (see Census) the couple had to pass through Samaria and into Judea, a long, dangerous and difficult three-day journey.

This trip had to be made over rough and often high ground. The nights were very cold, with only Joseph's thick coat of sheep's wool to keep Mary warm.

More and more people were going in the same direction, thus providing safety in numbers whilst the journey was under way. But the disadvantage of this situation was that overcrowding at the destination was inevitable and many people were forced to remain outside Bethlehem, huddled round smoky fires on the hillsides at night.

Joseph

Husband of Mary, Joseph had migrated from Bethlehem to Nazareth to follow his trade as a carpenter. He is portrayed as a kind and chivalrous man (Luke 1-5) and a caring father (Luke 2:16; Matthew 2:13). He must have died before the crucifixion, as there is no mention of him there.

Kings

The 'three Kings of the Orient' (the Wise Men, the Magi) are very mysterious figures. Suggestions that they came from Spain, Babylon and Africa have been complicated by their 'sightings' in Russia and Italy via the legends of Baboushka and Befana.

The mystery is compounded by their complete disappearance after their visit to Bethlehem.

The word 'magi' meant 'a group of astronomers' (hence their pursuit of 'the star'). Our word 'magic' comes from magi, and the suggestion of their wisdom and ability to see into the future probably derives from this.

The Kings have come to be known as Caspar, Melchior and Balthasar, and a final legend suggests that their remains were collected together and interred in Cologne Cathedral in 1190.

Light

This aspect of Christmas is covered in greater depth in the 'Links with other Cultures' section in this book.

Manger

As is mentioned in the notes on St Francis, cribs or manger scenes are now essentially portrayed as simple, humble affairs. This was not always the case. The original mangers in Middle Eastern countries were made of clay or stone. Their coldness was an obvious reason why Mary spread straw in the manger at Bethlehem so that the new-born child had warmth.

However, in the year 326 AD the Emperor Constantine built the Basilica of the Nativity, supposedly over the exact spot where Jesus was born. This established a pattern of cribs being bejewelled, ornate affairs. Francis considered this a travesty of the original and he re-established the simple cribs in the 12th century.

Mary

Mary, wife of Joseph and mother of Jesus, was also a native of Nazareth ('Miriam' in Hebrew) whose parents may have been Joachim and Anna. Mary spent three months with her relative Elizabeth before the birth of John the Baptist, in Judea. She then returned to Nazareth. Anna, her mother, is the patron saint of midwives.

Mistletoe

Mistletoe features in many legends but there are two which seem significant in its usage for decoration at Christmas time. One ancient thought was that because mistletoe's roots do not touch the ground it has magical qualities, therefore to decorate one's house with it was to ensure happiness and contentment.

In Norse legends Baldur was killed by Loki using mistletoe. Baldur eventually returned to life and promised that mistletoe could never hurt anyone again. As a result of this it came to symbolise love – and perhaps the practice of 'kissing beneath the mistletoe'.

Myrrh

Myrrh is the resinous substance derived from a spiny shrub found in Arabia. Its bitterness was symbolic because, in keeping with their reputation as being able to see into the future, the gift of myrrh from the Magi foretold of the bitterness and sorrow which awaited Jesus in later years.

Nazareth

Nazareth was the town in Lower Galilee from which Joseph and Mary began their journey to Bethlehem. A town of little importance, it was overshadowed by nearby Sepphoris in New Testament times. Nazareth was of course also the childhood home of Jesus.

Palestine

Part of the Roman Empire since 65 BC, Palestine had previously suffered at the hands of Assyria, Babylon, Persia and Greece. Not since the great days of David had the country enjoyed independent success. News of the birth of a 'new King' therefore generated great anticipation in the locals, and fear and suspicion in their rulers.

Pantomimes

These were originally performed only in the 'great houses' of the land. They had their origins in dance productions and were totally mimed. Despite the modern commercial influence which deems that popstars and 'celebrities' are now essential ingredients, the plots have remained basically the same – fairy stories in which good ultimately triumphs over evil.

In contrast to pantomimes, mummers' presentations were simply an opportunity for ordinary people to dress up, mime and dance. Again good always defeated evil and 'stock characters' like St George became very popular.

Paper chains

These originated with Victorian children in big industrial towns where evergreens were scarce.

Parcels and presents

In the not too distant past a parcel containing a Christmas present was referred to as a 'Christmas box'. Possible origins here relate to the opening of church poor boxes on 26 December when their contents were distributed to the poor of the parish, and also to the practice at Christmas time of medieval apprentices to visit their master's clients and friends carrying a box – into which they hoped to receive gifts of money.

Present giving was also a feature of the Roman Festival of Saturnalia (which began on 17 December and whose influence on Christmas customs is significant). Symbolic presents at this festival included honey, which promised a year of peace ahead; candles, which denoted a year of happiness and light; and money, which indicated a year of prosperity.

Robin

Perhaps the most significant bird associated with Christmas, he traditionally got his red breast from flying low over the fire in the stable at Bethlehem and fanning the flames to keep it alight. He was also a very prominent feature on Victorian Christmas cards. The latter were delivered by postmen who wore red coats and were themselves nicknamed 'robins'.

St Nicholas

An enormous amount of information exists about St Nicholas (the model for Santa Claus) but practically none of it can be confirmed as established fact. He was Archbishop of Myra in Asia Minor during the early fourth century. He is supposed to have died on 6 December between 345 and 355 (hence the significance of 6 December in the Christmas celebrations of so many European countries). In 1087 Italian seamen from Bari took the saint's remains from Myra back to Bari and a basilica was built to house them there. Fairly recent evidence however suggests that St Nicholas's remains were taken to the tiny island of Gemiler, off the coast of Turkey, in the 12th century. Although only half a mile long, the island has five decorated churches and a Byzantine complex apparently dedicated to St Nicholas.

From a children's point of view however St Nicholas was known for his friendliness and generosity. Of the many legends about him, the most appealing (and significant!) to the young was his practice of anonymously dropping gold pieces down the chimneys of poor young girls who were just about to be married.

Shepherds

'The Lord is my shepherd I shall not want' is just one statement which typifies the theme throughout the Bible linking leaders of the people with shepherds.

At a practical level, shepherds of the time wore an abayeh, a heavy cloak which protected them in all weathers. A fabric girdle contained money and pebbles which were thrown to attract the sheep's' attention. The shepherds' food, carried in a bag, was usually a simple mixture of cheese, olives, raisins and bread. He usually carried a 'rod', which was a thick club sometimes implanted with metal. This was used to beat off enemies and attackers of his sheep. His staff, for guiding the sheep was a longer thinner piece of wood.

In his book *The Historical Geography of the Holy Land*, George Adam Smith provides an evocative pen picture of a Judean shepherd:

'In such a landscape as Judea, where a day's pasture is thinly scattered over an unfenced tract of country, covered with delusive paths, still frequented by wild beasts, and rolling off into the desert, the man and his character are indispensable. On some high moor, across which at night hyenas howl, when you meet him, sleepless, far-sighted, weather-beaten, armed, leaning on his staff, and looking out over his scattered sheep, everyone of them on his heart, you understand why the shepherds of Judea sprang to the front in his people's history; why they gave his name to their King, and made him the symbol of Providence; why Christ took him as the type of self-sacrifice.'

Star of Bethlehem

Opinions about the 'star in the east' vary from those who consider it merely symbolic to those who think it was a miracle. Scientists offer three tentative suggestions: that it was an appearance of Halley's Comet; or a bright meteor; or a nova – an old star which, due to an internal explosion, suddenly burst into exceptional brilliance. All the speculations have doubts attached to them.

Stockings

The custom of hanging up a stocking on Christmas Eve originated with a delightful St Nicholas story. A wealthy man who enjoyed helping the poor, St Nicholas liked to perform his generous deeds with anonymity. Thus a present of gold to a poor peasant to help with his daughters' dowry was thrown into his house (down the chimney/through the window – sources vary!) and landed in a stocking which had been hung up by the fire to dry.

Traditionally stockings should contain some common features – a rosy apple was a bringer of good health; an orange in the heel was a luxury item because in the 19th century oranges were a very expensive fruit; a new penny was a forerunner of forthcoming wealth; a piece of coal symbolised warmth for the coming year.

Trees

The link between the Roman Saturnalia and the Christian Christmas is maintained in that Virgil mentions pine trees hung with decorations men used in the pagan feast.

Christmas trees originated in Germany and they were decorated with candles as far back as medieval times. The first Christmas tree in England is supposed to have been introduced by Queen Charlotte, wife of George III, at the beginning of the 19th century.

But, as with so many of our Christmas customs, it was the Victorians who made them the household feature they are today. Prince Albert, husband of Queen Victoria, is the person credited with making them so popular. He introduced one in Windsor Castle for the Christmas of 1841.

Wenceslas

'Good King Wenceslas looked out
On the Feast of Stephen,
Where the snow lay round about
Deep and crisp and even.'

The time to which we sing this familiar carol dates back to about 1250. The words are by a man named John Neale and date from the 19th century.

As well as being a king, Wenceslas was also a saint. As a very young man he became King of Bohemia in 921. Having been brought up in a monastery he was gentle and kind, qualities which made him very popular with his subjects. However they were cruel times and Henry I of Germany invaded Bohemia in 928. In order to avoid bloodshed Wenceslas welcomed the invaders into Prague. His brother, Boleslav, interpreted this as weakness and had Wenceslas murdered a year later.

The Czech people remember Wenceslas for his concern for his people and his many Christian acts. In Prague's Wenceslas Square his statue contains the following epitaph beneath it: 'St Wenceslas suffer not us nor our children to perish.'

Yule log

The Yule log was another feature with pagan origins. It was burned to encourage the dying sun of December to return again.

Zest

Zest is the peel of oranges and lemons, both of which are symbolic fruits at this time of the year. The lemon is the sign of faithfulness in love and the orange is a symbol of generosity. Both are associated with the Virgin Mary.

Maths for Christmas

2

(Activity sheets 3 – 12)

There are many aspects of Christmas which lend themselves to involvement with maths and work skills. For those teachers particularly interested in history then a study of old shopping catalogues and their prices offer an intriguing mix of social history and maths possibilities.

The Christmas shopping boom really began at the end of the last century. The department store Swears and Wells advertised 'mechanical marvels' such as the 'dancing cat' and the 'sociable pig'. There were musical toys. A very popular doll of this time was 'Dollie Daisy Dimple'. She could be yours, along with a trunk full of clothes for her and 'a little book about Miss Dimple's birthday and early history' for 5p (one shilling at the time).

'Number and Christmas' has plenty of possibilities today – via the calendar and number of days to the great occasion, cards sent and received by the children, presents sent and received, numbers of people invited to parties or involved in plays etc. 'Size and shape' feature in presents again and in the great variety of Christmas decorations, while calculation could involve the cost of these things. Father Christmas could be linked with direction finding and routes, and fractions occur in slicing cakes etc. Clocks and time are important in 'what we are doing and when' in the Christmas period and there is great scope for graphical presentation in showing who likes what best in carols, presents, food etc.

All of these features, and more, are used in the activity sheets which are associated with this chapter. There are ten of them.

(NB. The children could use the answer section of this chapter for self checking of worksheets if the teacher feels this is a useful exercise. Numbers are expressed in words and figures to give practice here.)

Sheet 3

The two patterns are:

○△▭▭○△▭▭○△▭▭○△▭▭ etc.

▭▭▭○△▭▭▭▭○△▭▭▭▭○△ etc.

Sheet 4

Number of stars = 8

Number of squares = 10

Number of rectangles = 12

Number of triangles = 15

Number of circles = 18

Number of shapes altogether = 63

Sheet 5

1 School ends on Friday.

2 Mummy's party is on a Saturday.

3 Letters to Father Christmas must be posted on a Tuesday.

4 Mummy ices the cake on a Thursday.

5 We are going to the pantomime on a Thursday.

6 Christmas Day is a Saturday.

7 There are 31 days in December.

8 The last day of the month is Friday 31 December.

Card 6

The shapes should be coloured in as follows:

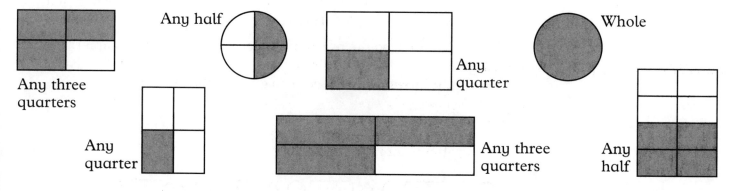

Sheet 7

1 Mandy woke up at 6 o'clock (am).

2 Mandy went to church at 9 o'clock (am).

3 Mandy was eating at 1 o'clock (pm).

4 Mandy was watching television at 3 o'clock (3pm).

5 Mandy went to bed at 7.30 (pm).

Sheet 8

1 I spend £9.
2 Two soldiers cost £2.
3 The cost of a ball, a book and a jigsaw is £6.
4 A doll, a tent and a skipping rope would cost £12.
5 A tent costs the most.
6 I could buy four toy soldiers for the cost of one engine.
7 A toy soldier, a jigsaw and a skipping rope cost the least.
8 All together these things would cost £23.

Sheet 9

1 Lee lives in Park Road.
2 Jill's house is in Ash Street.
3 Park Road.
4 Low Street (or a footpath).
5 Leroy and Delia live in Low Street.
6 Jill.
7 Leroy would cross Low Street.
8 There are five houses between Leroy's and Delia's.

Sheet 10

1 'Away in a Manger' is the best liked carol.
2 Rani likes 'O little Town of Bethlehem' best.
3 Two children like 'Little Donkey' best.
4 Harry, Mina and Rachid like 'Away in a Manger' best.
5 Rani does not like 'Away in a Manger' or 'Little Donkey'.

Sheet 11

1 Julie had the biggest present.
2 Daddy has the longest, thinnest present.
3 Paul's present is a triangle shape.
4 Grandad has the smallest present.
5 Gran's present has an oval top.
6 Five would be left.
7 Julie's present is $5\frac{1}{2}$ centimetres long.
8 Mum's present has six sides.

Sheet 12

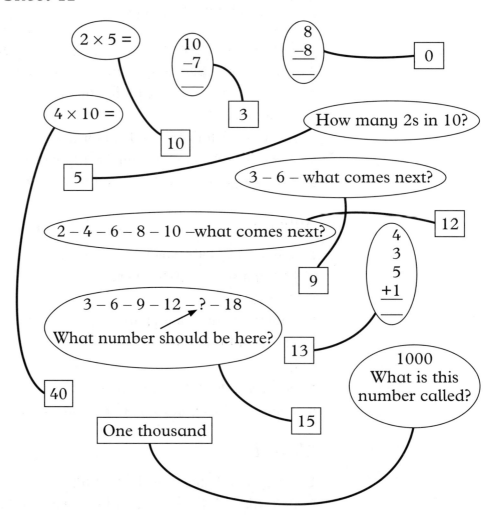

Christmas Language Activities

(Activity sheets 13 – 17)

Perhaps more than any other period of the year Christmas is a period associated with words and writing. Millions of Christmas cards are written and these often contain annual pieces of family information as well as the standard greeting.

Mum writes endless shopping lists and young children enjoy writing anticipatory letters to Father Christmas. Invitations to parties, direction-finding notes and (hopefully) thank you letters all add to the words written.

One of the main aims of this section, therefore, is to stimulate children's imagination by the writing and reading of letters, whilst at the same time giving some early experience of basic structure. One extra, and enormous, asset to this activity is the presence of computers in almost all classrooms. Both in the writing, correcting and presentation of letters this is a valuable resource.

The second half of the section moves on to activities like interviews and then the use of 'Christmas' in a variety of word games and activites.

There are five activity sheets linked to this work. The answers to the activity sheets are to be found at the end of the chapter.

Letters: starting points

An introduction to letters with young children could begin with the teacher producing one on the computer, writing one on the blackboard, or writing one in large print on a piece of card. Whichever way is used the idea is for all the class to focus on the letter and for ideas to develop from there. An additional practical point is that one letter on display will focus the children's attention on the format as well.

Perhaps the first requirement is to produce a letter which will give rise to some talking points, e.g.:

```
Billy Bonzo's Circus                              Class 7,
The Big Top,                            Cuckoo Lane School,
Bramley Moor,                                   Middlewitch
West Yorkshire.                                        Beds.


                                          1st December.

Dear Billy Bonzo,

Miss Pead is our teacher. She told us you are looking for a class of
children. You want them to work with the clowns in your Christmas show.

We would like to be this class! We can run and jump and roll about just
like you want.

It would be great fun.

Would you let us know if we can help?

          Best wishes,

          Class 7.
```

The teacher could then generate lots of talking points from this letter: What might happen at a circus? Why might Billy Bonzo want a group of children to work with the clowns? Would they dress up? If so, what in? Might they live with the circus – in caravans? What might they see, hear, feel, smell etc., at the circus?

At another level the questions might require a more prosaic study of the letter: Who is it addressed to? How does Billy Bonzo know who has written the letter? Does he know where to send his reply? How? Will he know when the letter was written? How? If the letter lost its envelope could it still reach Billy Bonzo? How?

Hopefully this talk will stimulate the children to want to write some letters of their own. Perhaps a good point at which to start here would be some 'letters to Father Christmas'.

The first of these might be a collective effort where ideas and suggestions are gathered together and reproduced on the computer. Such a letter might read something like the following:

```
Father Christmas                                    Class –
North Pole                              Chart Park School,
                                         Edenbridge Road
                                                Enfield,
                                    Middlesex EN1 5PD


                                           1st December

Dear Father Christmas,

It will soon be Christmas. Everybody in class is getting excited. We are
very busy, and we think you will be very busy too.

Is your sledge ready? Are your reindeers ready to pull it? Have you got
plenty of sacks to put all the toys in?

At school here we are going to have a Christmas party. We are doing a play
and our mums and dads are coming to see it. On the last day at school we
are having a Christmas dinner.

Yesterday it snowed. It was great. Of course you are used to lots of snow.
You have your big cloak to keep you warm.

That's all our news for now. We are all looking forward to you coming on
Christmas Eve. Don't get stuck in any chimneys.

        Love,

        from everybody in Class – .
```

From a teacher's point of view the great advantage of a collective letter to Father Christmas is that she can write and 'manufacture' a suitable and exciting reply. For instance with the help of a colleague the 'special delivery' of such a letter to the classroom could be arranged at a time to provide maximum impact.

For those teachers who feel their overworked imagination needs a boost then a dip into the wonderful *Father Christmas Letters* by J.R. Tolkien (originally published by Allen and Unwin in 1976) is a great stimulant.

The 'Father Christmas' reply letter might read something like the following:

                                                              Claus Castle,
                                                              North Pole,
                                                          10th December.

Dear Boys and Girls in Class – ,

I was very pleased to get your letter. I am glad you are having an exciting time at school.

Now what about my news? Did you know I lived in a castle? Well, I've got to because of all the room I need.

My castle is very, very big. It has four tall turrets and fifty rooms. There is a huge cellar. The windows are very small. There is a thick wooden drawbridge over the water round the castle. But the water is frozen. It is a huge sheet of ice! It is very, very cold at Claus Castle!

Most of the rooms in Claus Castle are for keeping presents for boys and girls. We've got the doll room and the train set room. We've got the book room and the computer room. We've got the football room and the skipping rope room.

Then we've got the surprise room. All the presents in there are surprises. Even I don't know what they are!

In the great hall we keep the sledges. They are the biggest sledges you've ever seen! I've got three. I use a different one each Christmas Eve. They are very heavy.

In the cellar we keep the sacks to put the presents in. We've got so many sacks they stretch from the floor to the roof! They are very thick and strong.

Outside is a big warm shed. Dasher and Dancer, my reindeers live in here. They are always hungry!

On Christmas Eve we load up the big sledge – sacks and sacks of presents. Then I put my warm red cloak on. Next come my big black boots. Then Dasher and Dancer are harnessed to the sledge and we thunder over the drawbridge. It is so exciting.

Next we pull slowly into the sky. We are coming to see you!

            So, until Christmas Eve,

            Love from Santa Claus.

(NB. Activity sheet 14 relates specifically to this letter. It would probably be most effective to use it immediately after reference to this letter.)

Letters: imagination and information

Another valuable use of letters is that, with a bit of imagination, they can pass on a great deal of useful information to the children. For instance, using the device 'a letter from the past' a child living in Bethlehem at the time when Jesus was born may have written an informative letter which has been 'discovered'. Such a letter might be as follows:

Bethlehem.

Dear Uncle Jacob,

Do you remember me? I am Ben. I am 7 years old now. I am writing to you because some very exciting things have been happening here.

The other day I was out in the town. It was very hot and crowded. Lots of people have come here to be counted. There are soldiers everywhere.

I help my mum and dad at our inn. I am fed up with making beds! Anyway, when it got dark on Tuesday night there was a great bang on the inn door.

'Help,' a man cried. 'Help, we need help.'

I looked out of my bedroom window. I saw a man, with a lady who was on a donkey. Then I heard my dad open the door.

'We've got no room here', he said. 'Try somewhere else.'

'There's nowhere left,' answered the man. 'Look, my wife's going to have a baby. We must have a room.'

'Please,' I heard the lady whisper.

'We've got no rooms,' said my dad again. 'But…'

I knew what was coming next.

'Ben!'

Five minutes later I was taking the man and his wife to our stable. They seemed very nice people.

'Thank you Ben,' said the lady when we got there.

Once they were in the stable with all the animals strange things started to happen. A load of shepherds came in from the hills. Then, when the baby was born, they gave him presents.

I was so tired I must have dozed off. But do you know I think some Kings even brought presents for the baby. And I heard singing.

But the best bit came just before morning. Mary, that was the lady's name waved me over. She showed me the new-born baby in the manger.

'This is Jesus, Ben', she said. 'And I want to thank you for your help tonight.'

I told you, Uncle – it has been very exciting here!

Love from

Ben.

Once again there are a great number of discussion possibilities which can follow on from this letter. (It has also been used as the basis of a play in the drama section of this book.)

It can be used to encourage the children to write some letters of their own to a distant relative (or imaginary) uncle, grandparent, cousin etc.

(NB. Activity Sheet 15 relates specifically to this letter. It would probably be best used immediately after reference to the letter section in this book. The answer could be used by the children for self correction. This would aid their appreciation of vocabulary and sentence construction.)

In these letters they could describe the 'build ups' to their own Christmases. Such letters might include diary type comments on preparations at home, activities at school, visits, shopping, special events and so on.

Whilst on this usage of letters for learning about and reflecting on past events, there was a marvellous story in the *Daily Telegraph* of 21 December 1996.

Peter Hulbert, a mechanic from Holt, near Trowbridge in Wiltshire was cleaning the chimney in his five year old son's bedroom. While he was doing so a pile of old sticks, nests and rubbish fell down into the grate. On top of this rubbish was a well preserved letter.

The letter was dated and this was helpful in finding that it had been written by Mabel Briggs, aged nine, on 8 December 1911! The contents of this letter caused a great impact when it was read to the children of the local school. It is reproduced here:

Holt, Wilts.
Dec. 8th 1911.

Dear Santa Claus,

Last year you brought me many nice presents and I think you were very kind indeed.

I expect you would like to know what I should like you to bring me this year.

Well, I should like you to bring me a storybook, a postcard album, a box of chocolates and a sweetshop.

We have a little baby and we would like you to bring her a little rattle that will blow.

Very soon we are giving a concert and we are learning some songs and you can come and hear them if you like.

I hope you will remember the very poor children in the slums and in the large towns.

I might stay awake for some time to see you come in our bedroom to put things in my stocking the night you come. Our house is on the common.

With much love,

I remain your friend, Mabel.

Research indicated that the sensitivity and concern for others which the young Mabel showed in this letter were qualities she carried into adult life.

The letter itself is a marvellous starting point for some historical considerations with young children. How might Mabel have been dressed? What would she have written the letter with? How have desirable Christmas presents changed? Why did she feel sorry for poor children who live 'in the large towns'? What situations have remained similar with those for today's children?

Moving from the historical to the fanciful, how fascinating the 'story of the letter' might be. When exactly was it written? Where was it written? How did it get up the chimney? What changes had it seen in the people who lived in the house – the village – the country? An historical 'time line' of events might draw these two aspects of work intriguingly together.

Asking questions

Interesting visitors to the classroom are a great asset at Christmas time. Some people's occupations are particularly relevant and/or busy at this time of the year. Those who might be included in this context are priests, postmen, shopkeepers, nurses, farmers, window designers, card creators, actors, actresses, carol singers etc. (Teachers too could claim inclusion.)

In a different context grandparents, people from other countries, those who have been in unusual places at Christmas (hospital, on board ship, on a trans-continental flight etc.) are others who could be very entertaining and informative.

The key factors in attracting visitors are of course their availability and interest, and the local knowledge of the school via its staff and children. With children of infant age the use of formal questionnaires which are often so successful with juniors is not really viable. It does help however if some 'questions' are worked out beforehand and various children are given the opportunity to ask them.

Here are some questions, which might be asked of the more predictable type of visitor. Obviously teachers will adapt the vocabulary to suit the specific needs of their classes.

Nurse
What hours might you work on Christmas day?

What do children who are in hospital get to eat?

Do they get presents like we do?

Are there Christmas decorations in the wards? Who puts them up?

Do you sing carols with the patients?

What about visitors on Christmas day?

Do you like working on Christmas day? Why?

Postman
What time do you get up in the morning? What time do you go to bed?

Do you make more deliveries at Christmas?

Do you have any extra help? Who gives you extra help?

How much heavier are your sacks?

What are most of the extra letters?

Have you had any strange parcels or letters to deliver?

Do you have many mistakes in addresses at Christmas? Why do you think these happen?

Is people's writing better/worse/the same at Christmas?

Why might there be a change here?

Do you like working at Christmas time?

What is your own Christmas day like?

Have any odd things happened to you at Christmas?

Shopkeeper (general store) or supermarket manager

Are you much busier at Christmas? Do you have to work much harder?

When do you have to start getting ready for Christmas? What do you have to do?

What sort of things do you sell most of?

Do people behave any differently when they are shopping at Christmas?

How do you make your shop/supermarket look more attractive at Christmas?

What sort of presents for others do people buy?

Are sweets and chocolates presented more attractively at Christmas?

How are comics and magazines different from normal?

Do you like working at Christmas?

How do you spend your own Christmas day?

Adult carol singer

When do you sing in public?

Where do you do your singing?

What carols do you sing? What carols are people's favourites?

How do you see the words if it is dark?

Do you have any instruments helping your singing?

Why do you sing carols? Why do you like singing them?

How do you make a collection?

Who gets the money you make?

How do people behave towards you?

Do you ever get invited into any houses?

Does anybody ever give you anything to eat or drink?

Elderly person

How long ago was it when you were a child at Christmas?

Did you go to church then?

What sort of presents did you get?

Was the food any different from what we eat today?

Was your house any different from today's houses?

What clothes did you wear on Christmas day?

What sort of games did you play at Christmas parties?

Do you enjoy Christmas now?

How do you spend Christmas day now?

What is the best way to enjoy Christmas?

Words and letters

Christmas word mate

A useful word activity which can be adapted for Christmas use is 'word mate'. For this the teacher needs to produce some cards containing single Christmas words. All of these single words can be linked with another on another card to give a correct pairing, e.g.

Card 1 Father *Card 2* Christmas.

The cards are then shuffled and distributed at random to the children. The latter then show their cards and pair off when they see their 'mate'.

Suggested 'mates' are:

Father Christmas; carol singers; Three Kings; Santa Claus; mince pies; Dasher Dancer; fairy lights; and then of course all the other words which go with 'Christmas' – party, tree, dinner, pudding, card, cracker, present, stocking, shopping, cake.

Christmas bingo

This is another simple, enjoyable activity which is excellent for encouraging letter/word recognition.

The teacher collects a range of pictures/photographs from newspapers and magazines (and her own drawings) and sticks these on a large piece of card. Subject matter might appear as follows:

snow scene	shopping	Santa Claus	children's party	Nativity scene	church	carol singers	chimney
balloons	decorating	sack	Xmas cake	stocking	holly	turkey	star
robin	Xmas card	lights	parcel	postman	shepherd	angels	school at Xmas
Xmas tree	reindeer	sleigh	toys	sweets	candle	advent calendar	cracker

The teacher then makes a series of smaller cards – each with appropriate words for one of the pictures. The word cards are distributed to the children and 'bingo' can be played in groups or as a whole class.

Who did what?

This is a useful language/recall game which can be played either in groups or with the whole class. In the context of this book it could be played after reading one or more of the stories.

If we take for instance 'Can You Help Father Christmas?' from the story section of this book, the sort of questions the teacher might pose for the class could be:

1 Who was very tired by delivering presents by himself?
2 Who said the sacks were heavy?
3 Who was old and wise?
4 Who were good at woodwork?
5 Who had an idea for making a sleigh?

6 Who was good at finding places but not very strong?

7 Who might wake children up whilst Father Christmas was in the chimney?

8 Who was 'chirpy'?

9 Who was shy?

10 Who said, 'Will you help on Christmas Eve'?

This 'who' formula can be applied to any well known story and children at the top end of Key Stage 1 could be encouraged to work out a sequence of questions themselves.

What comes next?

This game, which can be used with (or without!) specifically Christmas material, can be enhanced by introducing a competitive element.

The class could be divided up into four groups and asked to listen to a teacher's reading. This could be from a well known Christmas carol. For instance:

'Away in a ...'

The teacher stops immediately after 'a' and asks, 'What is the next word?' The first group to answer get a point and the game proceeds in the same manner.

Carols, poems, stories could all be used. Where the words are not familiar the game has the added advantage of demanding speculation about finding an appropriate word. This game not only focuses on vocabulary but demands vigorous concentration!

Activity sheet answers

The activity sheet entitled: 'A letter from Father Christmas' has no answer as such. Answers for the other cards related to this section are detailed below. It might be helpful for the teacher to let children use this book where self correction is thought advantageous.

Sheet 13

```
b  f  s  g  m  r  o  b  i  n
n  c  a  r  d  z  p  m  o  c
k  h  n  d  a  f  l  q  r  c
i  u  t  r  e  e  v  w  x  a
n  m  a  b  d  v  f  g  h  r
g  j  k  s  h  e  e  p  z  o
p  s  f  c  o  b  d  o  p  l
y  n  x  w  l  m  n  a  f  j
k  o  q  n  l  b  s  t  a  r
p  w  m  f  y  d  e  e  r  v
```

Sheet 15

1 Ben lives in Bethlehem.
2 The town was hot and crowded.
3 A man came to the door.
4 He wanted help.
5 Ben had to take the man and his wife to the stable.
6 Shepherds brought presents.
7 The baby's mother's name was Mary.
8 She said, 'This is Jesus, Ben'.

Sheet 16

Completed words in order are: carol, party, tree, crib, Santa, king, holly, card, star, robin, angel, present, snow, stocking, sack, cracker, Jesus, Mary, Bethlehem, candle, shepherd.

Sheet 17

The complete text for this card should read:

This is the story of a cat. His name is Mr Tibbs. On Christmas morning he walked into his house. He saw lots of parcels beside the (Christmas) tree. Then he saw something else. It was a basket. There was something in the basket. It was another cat!

'But I am the cat in this house!' said Mr Tibbs.

Just then Jessica came over and picked Mr Tibbs up.

'You are still the cat in this house,' she said. 'But now you have got a friend to play with you.'

Mr Tibbs wasn't very happy. Then he saw some milk in his bowl. He bent down and drank the milk.

Now he felt much better. He went to the basket. His friend was lying in it.

'Now,' said Mr Tibbs, 'What shall I call you? I shall call you . . . . '

Jessica saw the two cats looking at each other.

'I knew Mr Tibbs would like a friend for Christmas,' she said.

Creations and Investigations

(Activity sheets 18 – 21)

This chapter seeks to provide ideas for both of the above. The aim is to suggest a few ideas for class, group and individual activities and, at the same time, cater for those 'finishing early' for whatever reason. Included in the investigations are also ideas for removing some of the tedium in the inevitable 'clearing-up operations' which follow messy craft activities.

There are four activity sheets directly related to this section and these are mentioned specifically in the text in the context of appropriate pieces of work.

Decorating an infant school for Christmas is a very demanding task but one which teachers accomplish every year with astonishing verve and ingenuity. It is very much a contrast of 'big and small'. Large and colourful displays are needed for the hall, corridors and many parts of the classrooms. Small displays are needed in other classroom areas – and then there is the individual work of the children.

The first suggestions which follow here are 'big' ideas which are best suited for the hall, corridors or large display areas in classrooms.

'The Singers'
During December, and much to their delight, Key Stage 1 children usually learn to sing a number of carols – 'O Little Town of Bethlehem', 'Away in a Manger', Go Tell it on the Mountain', 'Little Donkey', 'I Want to See Your Baby Boy', 'Little Star', 'Mary had a Baby' etc.

A very effective display for hall or corridors is to portray groups singing these carols, with a few words from them and a chosen scene pictured, as supplements. The singers could be portrayed by painting a group of children's faces and then sticking some facsimile 'music' in front of the lower half of each face. The 'music' would only be stuck to the picture by its extreme ends and thus the spine of each sheet gives a 3D effect.

For example:

A-B, C-D, on each piece of 'music' is where the card/paper is stuck to the picture itself.

Once the groups of carol singers are in place then some of the words from the carol they are singing could be printed above them. A small scene from the carol might then be illustrated to one side of the main picture.

Various groups/scenes like this in hall or corridor are colourful, look more sophisticated than their relatively simple construction requires, and are an aid to reading too!

The Twelve Days of Christmas

This poem is reproduced in the poems and prose section of this book and its repetitive nature is a useful counting exercise for young children – and one which they enjoy immensely. Again to illustrate each verse in a progressive manner makes this an ideal arrangement for a long corridor, or a circuit round a hall or dining room.

A variety of media could be used here and further dramatic effects could be obtained by some 3D work and even simple sound effects. Suggestions might include:

The partridge in the pear tree could 'appear' in a large background tree, with a 3D collection of 'leaves and pears' stuck to it. Turtle doves could be at the entrance to a dovecote and a tape of doves 'cooing' could be played at regular intervals here. The latter might have been made by the children in a sound effects session.

The three French hens could be a mixture of card and wool, whilst the colly birds could be material with sparkling button eyes. The gold rings might be a selection of perhaps parentally supplied earings, mounted on a felt or velvet background. The geese-a-laying could show the geese in the background but the scene might be dominated by a shelf of large, papier maché eggs.

The swans-a-swimming could be cut outs of white card superimposed on an all-blue background, and the milk maids could be created by materials stuck onto the outlines of the figures.

Drummers drumming could be dominated by a life size painting of a drummer. Attached to the picture at an appropriate point could be either one of the school's drums or one which has been borrowed. Real drumsticks would add to the effect as would another regularly played tape of drumming here.

The pipers piping could be a straightforward piping/marching picture and all those exotic pieces of material which all infant classrooms seem to have could be put to good use for the ladies dancing. Once again some waltz music to supplement this scene would add to the fun.

Finally the lords-a-leaping could be a photograph montage from magazine/newspaper cut-outs. Figures of sportsmen leaping – via football, athletics, basketball, swimming etc. – are not hard to find and would make a dramatic final scene.

Obviously many teachers will have their own ideas of how to build up a 'Twelve Days' sequence like this but however it is done the children will enjoy it. Similarly the sound effects approach will vary. Obviously all would not want to be played at once and various children might be given the task of activating different sounds when required.

Silhouettes

Once again for a long corridor or hall wall a silhouette picture is both dramatic and interesting. The background couldn't be easier to arrange – simply unroll some long strips of various tissue paper and stick or pin this in place on the display board. Some overlap of the colours adds to the effect.

The scene is then set for the silhouettes. These could be of various Christmas features – shepherds, sheep, kings, stable, manger etc. Or more modern features such as church, carol singers, Christmas trees.

Hoop show

Finally in this sub-section, the use of hoops from the school's PE equipment is another aid to 'big' display. Once the hoops have been decorated they could then be hung from the hall or corridor roof to give attractive points.

The first aspect of their decoration could be the covering of the hoop itself with attractively coloured tissue paper. The appeal is then to decide what to put in the circle within. Pictures reflecting the 'Twelve Days of Christmas' is one possibility, another is to have the rings displaying scenes/characters from pantomimes. 'Christmas food' is another possibility with plenty of ingenuity often shown here.

One idea, which is purely visual and not 'themed' is to decorate each hoop with a number of dangling fir cones. Once a collection of the latter has been made they could first of all be painted, and then sprayed with gold or silver glitter. Various lengths of strong thread could then be attached to each cone so that they could hang within the hoop. E.g.

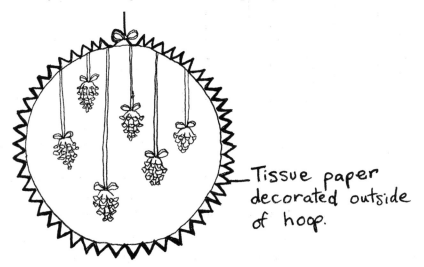

Tissue paper decorated outside of hoop.

The next group of suggestions are firmly classroom based but the end products are again the total of many hands.

Advent calendars

There is one social aspect to consider right from the start here. Advent calendars traditionally have 24 windows to open – but most infant classes these days have more than 24 children in them. One way round this issue is to have the children open the doors in pairs, with other guests being invited to come into the classroom (admire the calendar!) and open a door. Such guests might include the headteacher, secretary, caretaker, school crossing lady, cook etc.

One advent calendar suggestion would be to base it on 'Santa's castle', which is a feature in other parts of this book. The preparation would be as follows:

Requirements
One piece of thick white card, another piece of thin white card of the same size

Pencils, rulers, glue, paste

Coloured sticky backed paper

Paint

A Stanley knife for the teacher's use

A selection of old Christmas cards

Technique
Carefully measure and draw the castle on the thick sheet of card, putting all the windows in place:

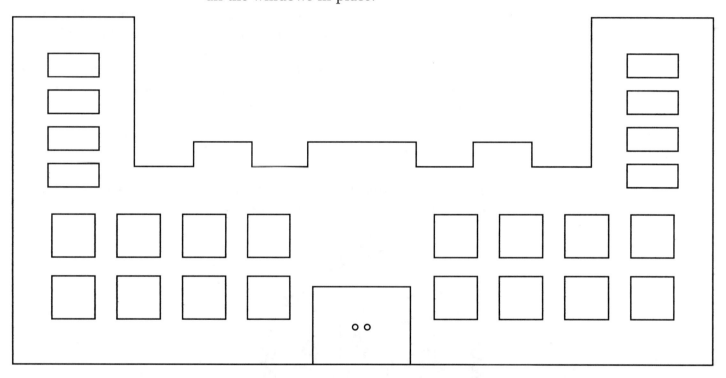

When the castle is in place like this on the thick card, make a selection of attractive pictures, shapes and colours from the old Christmas cards. Cut these out and glue them onto the windows of the castle.

Now take the piece of thinner white card and reproduce castle shape and windows so that these fit exactly over their counterparts on the thick card.

Next, prepare the windows on the thin, cover card.

With ruler and stanley knife, cut along A – B, C – D, and X – Y.

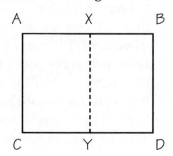

The windows will now open outwards from X – Y. Use ruler to get a straight opening edge.

Now stick the thin card with the opening windows on top of the thick card. Check that windows are perfectly aligned before sticking, and stick down with them slightly open so that no glue inadvertently gets into their backs.

Once the cards are stuck together then some imagination can be brought to bear in decorating the front of Santa's castle. Blocks of 'stone' could be painted on and covered with creepers; there might be a snow-covered facade. Once this is complete then numbers could be cut from the coloured sticky-backed paper and stuck on the windows. From all points of view it seems better if these numbers are stuck on in a random way. These lead to an exciting search, and an enhanced counting exercise before the correct window is located.

Lighting up time

This is an enjoyable and creative construction which is highlighted by being able to illustrate it. Useful science is also involved in arranging the circuit to 'light up' the model.

Requirements

Cardboard box with detachable lid

Card for making cut-out figures, furniture, tree etc.

Paint, ruler, Stanley knife, scissors

Electrical equipment – battery, bulb, switch circuit

Technique

Remove the lid from the cardboard box. Paint the inside of the lid as if it is a ceiling in a house. Paint the rest of the box as if it is a decorated room in a house. (Old wallpaper pattern books are useful instead of paint here – if they are available.)

Design, paint and cut out figures, furniture, a Christmas tree to go in the house to represent a scene at Christmas in a modern house.

As for the 'Santa's castle' advent calendar cut out a viewing window at the lengthy end of the box, eg.

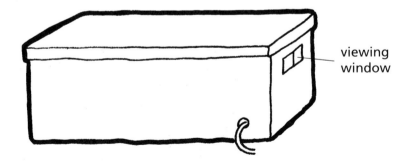

viewing window

Next cut a small hole in the box for the wires to pass through. Put the people in the box. Put the light bulb in the box, placed beneath viewing window. Connect up the wires – bulb – battery – switch. Put the lid firmly back on the box.

The whole thing is now set up for viewing. When this is done the viewer opens the window and then switches on the light, illuminating the scene within.

There are several possible offshoots here. Discussion and experiment as to where best to place the light is a very useful exercise. Other boxes could be set up. These might reveal things such as: the Nativity scene, a room in Santa's castle, a Victorian family at Christmas, the inside of a church, 'our classroom' and so on. There is a great deal of scope here.

Stained glass windows

There are many techniques for providing stained glass windows in the classroom but the one described here falls into the categories of 'big, bold and simple'.

Requirements
Plastic film (or plastic bags)
Felt tipped pens
Tissue paper
Thinned out adhesive (marvin medium)

Technique
Decide on the number and size of windows to be covered. Decide on the pattern/figures/scenes to appear on the windows. Produce these in outline, with felt tips on the plastic. Fill in the outlines with coloured tissue paper.

Presents for all

This is a 'present from Santa' exercise in which it is possible to mix craft and a little historical interest for the enjoyment of all.

Requirements
Two or three fairly large empty cartons (ice cream?)
Polyfilla
Coloured cotton and tissue paper
Two or three fairly large twigs
Gold or silver paint spray
A selection of rings (cheap!), thimbles, buttons, coins

Technique
Fill the cartons with a $2\frac{1}{2}$ to 1 polyfilla and water mix respectively. After an hour to an hour and a half, 'set' a substantial twig in each carton. Leave overnight so that the mix hardens thoroughly.

Wrap the objects, buttons etc. in the tissue paper. Make sure that there is enough for every child in the class to get one. Avoid their 'shape' giving away what is inside.

Spray the whole carton setting – carton, mix, twig – with silver or gold spray.

Using bright coloured cotton thread attach the tissue-wrapped objects to the twig. Mix these up thoroughly before putting them on the tree so that no-one has any idea what is in each.

Things are now ready for the next stage and the teacher might like to reflect on how to use this. The basic historical link here is with the Victorians, who loved tiny objects 'discovered' at Christmas and liked to see them as symbols for their personal futures.

For instance those who received rings would be married quickly, whereas the receipt of a thimble foretold an old maid. A button meant a man would remain a bachelor, but anybody getting a coin (it was originally a sixpence) would become rich. The teacher might like to discuss these things with the children before the objects are indiscriminately picked by them – but she might decide to have different symbolic interpretations to avoid any hurt feelings!

As can be seen there is again plenty of scope for development here, with all kinds of small objects being used – and being given a variety of imaginative meanings.

The craft suggestions which follow at this point will result in pieces of work for individual children.

CHRISTMAS CARDS

'The surprise package'
The idea behind this card is to produce a fold-up card which can be delivered in an envelope. The card itself then opens up to reveal the message inside. Instructions of how to make this simple card are detailed here, and Activity Sheet 18 is a template which can be used by the children to make the card.

Requirements
Thin card or stiff paper

Crayons, felt tips (perhaps a picture to stick in)

Ruler

Scissors

Envelope

Technique
The basic shape of the card is as follows. Measurements may vary but proportions must remain the same. The end product, when folded, should fit into an envelope.

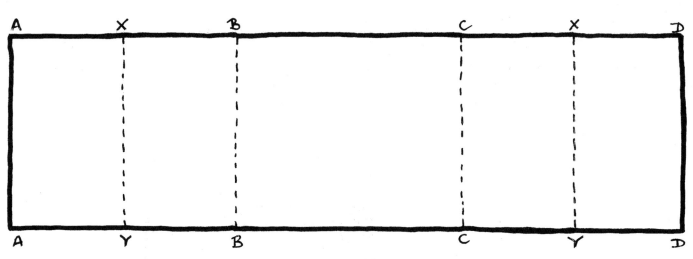

Fig. 1

A to B, B to C, C to D, should all be equidistant.

XY is half way between AB and CD.

The dotted lines indicate where folds have to be made.
(N.B. Dotted lines are simply for folding guidance and should be very faint.)

The next step is to cut out this figure. A to X is then folded so that A to X is on the outside. X – B is folded so that it is on the inside. The same applies to the other half of the figure. It should now look like this:

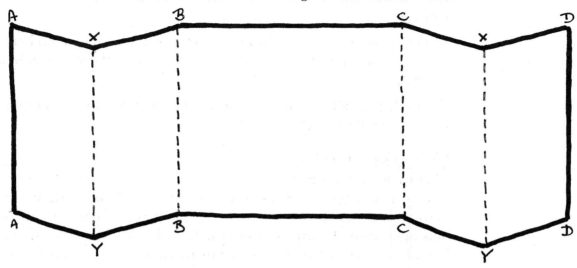

Fig. 2

Flatten the card out again. Draw (or stick in) a Christmas scene and message in the section X – B – C – X.

Then draw two ends of a cracker in the sections A – X; X – D, and colour them in.

This should appear as:

Fig. 3

Edges of the outside 'cracker handle' could be cut out.

The inside of the ragged edge is left crayoned in to give the appearance of a cracker which has just been pulled.

The card is then re-folded as in fig. 2 and put in an envelope. Prior to opening it should appear:

Fig. 4

The picture card

Requirements

Card, white paper

Felt tip

Scisssors, ruler, glue

Paper punch and gold or silver thread

Technique

Take a piece of coloured card. Cut to required size. Lay it out flat. Cut a piece of white paper, slightly smaller – to go inside, e.g.

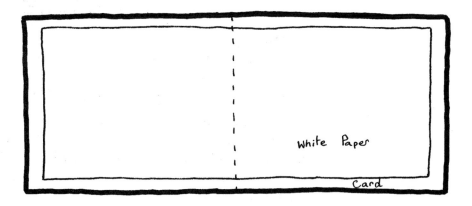

Fold the two over very carefully to make a card, with an 'inside'. Punch two holes in as shown and tie through holes with gold or silver thread:

The basic card now exists to be developed as and how the child or teacher decides. If a frame is carefully drawn on the front of the card a photograph of the sender could be lightly glued into this frame to give the card a definite personal touch.

'Big present' tags

Young children thoroughly enjoy giving presents, and if their personal stamp is obvious on the gift it gives them added pleasure.

The two ideas which follow are for large present tags and the templates for these can be found respectively on Activity Sheets 19 and 20.

King tags

This is simply an outline of a king (as seen on the sheet) which can be filled in to give a 3D effect. Pieces of material can be stuck on the section cloak: wool could be used for beard and hair; gold card could depict crown and gift container. Hands and face could be painted.

A hole could then be punched in part of the cloak and the gift card could be threaded to the figure with coloured thread. If the figure needs stiffening then a piece of thicker card the same shape could be stuck on the back, e.g.

Santa tags

Activity Sheet 20 contains the basic outline for this figure. It can be crayoned before being cut out and again 3D effects can be achieved with cotton wool for beard, material for cloaks buttons, etc.

The card is then cut out, bent round and stuck with the flap. A hole can then be punched somewhere on the cloak. Through this hole could be threaded an attractively coloured cotton/wool which is attached to the greetings label. The whole thing could then be placed on top of a small present, or act as the 'headpiece' for a bottle.

Enlarge the photocopy for larger Santas!

Face, beard, buttons, painting etc. all to be added and done before figure is cut out and stuck.

Present boxes

Having made two large present tags young children also enjoy going to the other extreme and working on something very small. Sheet 21 contains a simple cut-out shape for making a 'present box'. Obviously some help with cutting, bending and glueing will be needed here but the decoration of the box shape before these activities could be left entirely to the children. The lid could then be left open until the present – a sweet, small piece of inexpensive jewellery, decorative hair clip – is put inside. The lid could then be sealed.

From a construction point of view it is best to glue flap A to B first and let this thoroughly dry. Folds are best done along the edge of a ruler. Again, enlarge the copy to make a larger box.

Investigations

An infant classroom is a very busy place when 'creations' are in progress by groups or individuals. Like all activities however there is the situation where some groups finish earlier than others. In this context, and again with Christmas as the motivating theme, if some investigative material has been set up in advance then this can be both interesting and educationally beneficial for those finished early, waiting for glue to dry, just come back from absence etc.

Four such activities are described here. All are easy to set up and require little in the way of materials.

Investigation 1: *Santa's sledge trip*

A simple, basic street plan could be drawn on thick paper. An imaginary house could then be selected and a marker put over this spot. This marker could contain one of the children's names, eg:

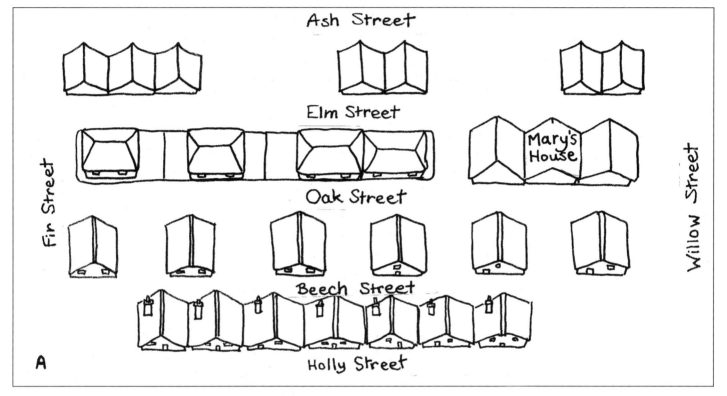

The question could then be posed: 'How can Santa find Mary's house?' starting off from point A.

A paper clip (Santa's sledge) could then be positioned on point A. A magnet could then be used underneath the paper to 'guide' the paper clip to the appropriate house.

There are any number of possibilities for developing this game. The marker, bearing another child's name, could be put on any number of different houses, requiring another route to be followed.

One child could be the 'sledge driver' whilst another gives directions – 'straight along Holly Street, left at the end into Willow Street, left at Oak Street, third house along on the right'. Alternative routes to the same destination could be discussed in terms of longer, shorter, quicker, slower etc.

This game is great fun and yields much valuable work.

Investigation 2: *A Christmas 'lucky dip'*

This investigation maintains the magnetic theme. Fill a shallow tray with sand and bury in it a selection of paper clips, screws, nuts. The children, in turn, then trawl the sand with a magnet until they have found something.

This can be played on a competitive game basis – each child has 15 seconds (recorded on a stop watch) for trawling. If he or she gets anything then they get a point.

Developments can include the addition of other objects – buttons, hairpins, matchsticks etc. – to test which materials are attracted to the magnet.

Investigation 3: *Toys from last Christmas*

In preparation for this game each of the children could be asked to bring in one of their toys from home. The teacher's contribution would need to be an old pillow case or bag with a drawstring neck.

Once they are all in the classroom the toys could be set out in a permanent display in December. Various investigations might then be related to them.

The first one might be a group activity as follows. One child selects a toy and puts it in the bag – none of the others in the group are allowed to see this. When the toy is in the bag, the latter is passed round the round. On the first round the children are only permitted to feel the toy through the bag and each child describes what he or she can feel – hard, sharp, round edges, soft, squeezy etc. When everybody has given their description each offers an opinion as to what the toy is. If all answers are wrong then the exercise is repeated, but this time the children are allowed to feel (but not look!) inside the bag.

For the second game the teacher could determine a number of words which a child could use to describe one of the toys on display – eg. 'Big, red, moves on wheels'. The others could then be invited to work out the answer from the description, with the winner then going on to another description, and so on.

A third activity could be to group the toys into sets – which ones move on wheels, which ones are red, which ones make a noise, which ones are soft – and so on. A drawing activity could include children choosing to draw one of the toys without saying which it is. When completed everyone has to guess what the others have drawn.

Investigation 4: *Clearing up*

So often the clearing and washing up after craft sessions is a chore for both teacher and children. If however an 'investigation' into clearing up is instituted then things can be much more interesting.

For instance the class would be divided into groups and each given a selection of paint brushes to clean. The groups could have different materials-

1 cold water only in a bowl

2 warm water in jars

3 warm water with some soap powder and jars

4 all that (3) have and a drying cloth

Obviously materials – and things to be cleaned – could vary but the final discussion on each occasion could be – which group achieved the best results, and why did they do so?

This is also a good idea to use after the class Christmas party. Keep some of the debris back until the next morning and have a well organised cleaning and testing session with results of 'how which and why' carefully recorded.

'Now Listen to This ...': Some Christmas Poems and Stories

5

(Activity sheets 22 – 23)

This section contains a varied offering of poems and stories which are aimed particularly at Key Stage 1 children.

The Twelve Days of Christmas

Every Key Stage 1 teacher knows how much young children enjoy repetition! They find this Christmas poem great fun – particularly if the class is split up into twelve pairs or groups so that each pair can have 'their' line throughout – 'four turtle doves' or 'three French hens' or whatever. The poem is equally enjoyable whether said to a clapping rhythm or sung to the traditional tune.

A suggestion in the 'Creations and Investigations' section of this book details how the words of 'The twelve days of Christmas' can be used to stimulate a large scale display.

On the first day of Christmas
My true love sent to me,
A partridge in a pear tree.

On the second day of Christmas
My true love sent to me
Two turtle doves
And a partridge in a pear tree.

On the third day of Christmas
My true love sent to me
Three French hens,
Two turtle doves
And a partridge in a pear tree.

On the fourth day of Christmas
My true love sent to me
Four colly birds ...
etc.

On the fifth day of Christmas
My true love sent to me
Five gold rings ...
etc.

On the sixth day of Christmas
My true love sent to me
Six geese-a-laying ...
etc.

On the seventh day of Christmas
My true love sent to me
Seven swans-a-swimming …
etc.

On the eighth day of Christmas
My true love sent to me
Eight maids-a-milking …
etc.

On the ninth day of Christmas
My true love sent to me
Nine drummers drumming …
etc.

On the tenth day of Christmas
My true love sent to me
Ten pipers piping …
etc.

On the eleventh day of Christmas
My true love sent to me
Eleven ladies dancing …
etc.

On the twelfth day of Christmas
My true love sent to me
Twelve lords-a-leaping …
etc.

Traditional

Shoes for Christmas

Harry didn't like his own shoes. But he liked Dad's wellies. And Mum's high heels. And brother Howard's football boots.

He even liked Grandad's gardening shoes. And Gran's keep-fit trainers. Most of the time Harry was wearing somebody else's shoes. And that's how it all began...

The doorbell rang one morning. It was nearly Christmas. Everybody was getting parcels.

'Postman!' shouted Harry, looking out of the window.

'Coming,' called Mum.

'Parcel,' said the postman. Mum took it and closed the door.

'What is it?' asked Harry.

'I don't ... oh, it's not for us.'

Mum looked at the label. 'It's for a Mr. U. Kando. Must be a mistake. I'll leave it here and give it back to the postman tomorrow.'

Mum put the parcel down. She went into the kitchen.

Harry could see a little tear in the parcel's wrapping.

He poked a finger in. The tear got bigger ... and bigger.

Now he could see inside.

Yes ... there was no doubt about it.

In the parcel was ... a pair of shoes!

Harry tore off a little more paper. And a little more. Then, putting his hand inside, he pulled out the shoes.

He had never seen anything like them.

They were small, black and shiny. A red wiggly line went all round them. The laces were a bright yellow. There was a silver arrow on each toe. They were the best shoes Harry had ever seen!

Slowly he squeezed his foot into one of them. It was a perfect fit! He put the other shoe on – and then it happened!

Suddenly he found himself standing up. His feet began to tingle in the shoes. Chisel the cat shot out of the room. Old Roger the dog crept behind the settee.

Then Harry's right foot began to tap up and down. His left foot did the same. He was dancing ... up and down ... faster and faster.

'Whee!' cried Harry.

Faster and faster the shoes danced. Across the room, over the chairs. Up the walls. On the ceiling.

'Whoaa!' he cried.

Roger put his paws over his head. 'Crazy kids,' he growled.

Back down the walls danced Harry. Over the chairs, across the room. The shiny black, red, yellow and silver shoes started to slow down. Then they stopped.

'Ooooh,' gasped Harry. Roger looked out from under a paw. Chisel peeped round the door.

'Ooooh,' said Harry again. 'Got to get these shoes off.'

He put one hand down. He tried to pull off a shoe. It was too tight. He couldn't move it. Then ... the tingling started again!

'AAAh,' cried Harry.

In a flash he was through the front door. In the street the shoes began to run. Harry ran past Jessica, the girl next door. She was going to nursery school with her mum.

'Harry!' shouted Jessica, waving her lolly. 'Harry!'

But Harry couldn't shout back. The shoes were going too fast. Faster and faster they went.

Now Harry was running beside a bus. The passengers stared at him. Their mouths opened wider and wider as Harry raced past them.

He shot past the supermarket where all the Christmas decorations glistened. Then he raced past the garage where Dad got his petrol. A man filling his car dropped the petrol pump as Harry rocketed by.

'Cor!' he gasped. 'Cor – what was that?'

Harry shot into the park. Two dogs saw him coming. Barking and bounding they chased him. But of course they couldn't catch him.

'Not fair,' growled one.

'No,' panted the other. 'Kids running faster than dogs. That's not fair!'

On sped Harry. He raced into the children's play park. He ran up the slide – and down the other side.

Then the shoes suddenly stopped. Harry nearly shot out of them.

Swish. They turned round and began to run again, back the way they had come.

'Oooh…aaah' cried Harry. His legs were getting very tired!

Through the park. Past the garage. By the supermarket. Along the street. On and on the shoes raced until – suddenly – Harry was home again.

Roger and Chisel watched from behind the settee.

'Oh….oh…er,' said Harry, all of a flutter. 'Got to get these shoes off.'

He put one hand down.

He tried to pull off a shoe.

Roger growled.

Harry couldn't move the shoe. It was too tight.

'Oh no,' he cried.

Chisel hid under a cushion.

The tingling in the shoes started again!

Then they started jumping. Up and down, up and down. Then Harry was outside again.

Up and down. Faster and higher.

At first Harry's jumps were as high as the hedge.

'Look at that. Wish I could jump like that,' shouted an old lady, pointing her stick at Harry. 'I could when I was his age.'

But Harry's jumps got higher … and higher.

Whizzing up in the air he looked down on the roofs of cars. Then he saw Jessica again. She was at the nursery school gate.

'Jess…' Harry called.

But the next jump took his breath away.

Up and over the nursery school he went.

'Mum,' shouted Jessica. 'There's Harry. He's flying.'

'Don't be silly, and stop picking your nose,' said her mum.

'OOOoooh,' cried Harry. He could hardly breathe. One minute he was whizzing up. Next he was dropping so fast his hair stood on end.

Now he was outside the town's football ground. Up he went. Past the grandstand. Past the floodlights. The practising players looked tiny on the field below.

'Never mind what's up there,' shouted the trainer. 'Watch the ball.'

Down and down came Harry. Then, with short fast jumps the shoes raced home again.

Soon Harry was inside once more.

Roger and Chisel were hiding under the carpet. Only their heads were sticking out.

'He's back again,'growled Roger.

'Yeah – watch it,' hissed Chisel.

'Must ... must ... must get these shoes off,' puffed Harry.

He got hold of the shiny, black red, yellow and silver shoe.

He pulled and tugged.

Suddenly – it came off!

Quick as a flash Harry pulled the other shoe off.

Then, as if they'd never been out, the shoes were back in the parcel. There was only a little tear in the wrapping.

Just then Mum came into the room.

'You still here Harry,' she said. 'What have you been doing?'

'She'd never believe him,' growled Roger, head under his paws again.

But Harry said nothing.

And do you know – from that day he never EVER looked in anybody else's Christmas parcel again!

Snapdragon

(Before the reading of this poem the children will enjoy hearing about what it refers to. Following the great Christmas feasts of Victorian times, after-dinner activities included the playing of many parlour games. One of the most spectacular of these was 'Snapdragon'. A pewter dish was put on the floor and filled with brandy. The brandy was then set on fire and currants were scattered in the dish. The players had to snatch the currants from the blaze and put them in their mouths – putting out flames by doing so. Obviously such a game was played mainly in well-to-do households!)

Here he comes with flaming bowl,

Don't he mean to take his toll,

Snip! Snap! Dragon!

Take care you don't take too much,

Be not greedy in your clutch,

Snip! Snap! Dragon!

With his blue and lapping tongue
Many of you will be stung,
Snip! Snap! Dragon!
For he snaps at all that comes
Snatching at his feast of plums,
Snip! Snap! Dragon!

But old Christmas makes him come.
Though he looks so fee-fo-fum.
Snip! Snap! Dragon!
Don't ever fear him, but be bold
Out he goes, his flames are cold.
Snip! Snap! Dragon!

Anon

Juan and Maria's Gift

(The Mexican story of the Christmas poinsettia has several versions and re-tellings but its effectiveness with young children is enduring.)

Juan and Maria were twins. They lived in a village in Mexico and they were very poor.

'It'll soon be Christmas,' said Maria one day. 'What are we going to take as presents for Baby Jesus this year?'

Juan's long dark hair fell over his eyes as he shook his head.

'Well... I don't know, but I'm sure we'll think of something,' he replied, trying to sound more cheerful than he felt.

The family was so poor that there was barely enough money for food, and certainly none for buying presents.

Christmas got nearer and Juan and Maria talked about the great procession which went through the village on Christmas Eve. Everybody in the village walked in the procession and when they got to the church they gave their gifts to the priest.

Then Juan had an idea.

'Maria – I've got it,' he exclaimed. 'We'll collect two pieces of wood and I'll carve two angels. Then we can have one each to give to the priest.'

'Oh Juan, what a wonderful idea,' gasped Maria. 'And you're such a good carver I'm sure they'll look lovely.'

Next day the twins found two good pieces of wood. Then Juan started work. He spent hours chipping, shaping and smoothing the wood until two figures of angels began to take shape. Maria helped him to paint them and they looked beautiful.

'You've done a very good job there,' said the twins' mother proudly. 'Anybody would be pleased to give a present like that.'

Soon the great day came, Christmas Eve. The whole village was alive with excitement. Old Pablo and his musicians played in the village square, girls got out their best dresses and everybody got their gifts ready to take in the procession.

Eventually darkness fell over the village, but lights twinkled everywhere.

The square was packed with people. Many carried candles and there was singing and music as the great procession began to form up.

'Keep tight hold of our angels, ' warned Juan as he held his sister's hand and tried to see past the adults who were pushing all round him. The crowd was so big that he had a job just keeping his feet on the ground.

'Juan ... Juan!'

Maria's voice suddenly sounded frightened.

'It's all right,' said Juan. 'I'll look after you.'

'No, no,' gasped his sister. 'I've dropped them.'

Juan could feel his mouth dry up and his head starting to pound. If Maria had dropped the fragile wooden angels in this crowd, then...

Pushing at the passing adult legs the twins searched for their gift. For minutes they could see nothing ... and then Juan saw a little parcel lying on the ground. Even as he watched heavy feet pounded over it.

Thrusting through the crowd he snatched the package up. Slowly he opened it and, as he did so, Maria let out a long, low cry.

The two angels were now just smashed peices of wood.

In one hand Juan held the wreckage of his work; in the other he clasped his tearful sister.

'Oh Juan, I'm so sorry. What are we going to do?'

'Well,' replied Juan. 'These are no good anymore – and I haven't time to make anything else. But we must take something as our gift to Jesus.'

By now most of the procession had left the village square and was on its way to church. Looking round Juan saw only the scruffy, weed-like bush which grew all over the village. Without a word, he knelt down and carefully broke a piece of it.

Then, still holding Maria's hand, he hurried after the crowd. At the church people slowly moved up to the manger and handed their gifts to the priest. The twins, covered in dust from their searching, and looking very poor in their old ragged clothes, were last in the line.

When they reached the priest they held out together the piece of bush. Looking at their sad faces the priest realised that this was not the gift they had intended to give.

'Thank you, my children,' he said kindly, as he reached out to take the twins' gift. But then ... even as the priest's hand was stretching out ... something amazing happened!

At the end of each branch of the piece of bush a flash of colour suddenly appeared. It got brighter as one beautiful red, star-shaped flower after another blossomed.

The people in the church gasped as they saw what was happening. The twins' gift had been the most wonderful of all.

Stir-about

Into the basin
put the plums.
Stir-about,
Stir-about,
Stir-about.

Next the good
white flour comes.
Stir-about,
Stir-about,
Stir-about.

Sugar and peel
And eggs and spice.
Stir-about,
Stir-about,
Stir-about.

Mix them and fix them
and cook them twice.
Stir-about,
Stir-about,
Stir-about.

Anon

Can You Help Father Christmas?

Did you know that a long, long time ago Father Christmas used to deliver presents on Christmas Eve – all by himself, without any reindeer or sledge? He found this very tiring indeed. The sacks were terribly heavy and he had so many homes to visit he sometimes got lost.

'What I need is some help,' he sighed to himself, after one particularly tiring Christmas.

So he sent for all the animals he knew. Along they came to Claus Castle. There were dogs, cats, birds, bears; dozens of animals young and old, big and small. Father Christmas spoke to them.

'My friends,' he said. 'I love my job. Taking presents to people on Christmas Eve is wonderful – but I need some help to do it better.'

'You're right,' barked a giant polar bear. 'I don't know how you manage to carry all those heavy sacks for a start.'

'Hmm,' muttered a wise old owl thoughtfully. 'Why don't you carry all the presents in a sleigh?'

'What a marvellous idea!' gasped Father Christmas. 'The gnomes who live in the village are very clever at making things like that.'

'Yes,' agreed a shaggy St Bernard dog, 'and you can use last year's Christmas trees to make a really good sleigh.'

'I knew you'd have some good ideas!' said Father Christmas excitedly clapping his hands. 'That's a ... oh dear.'

'What's the matter?'

'Well, a great big sleigh full of presents – I'll never be able to pull it.'

The animals were silent.

Father Christmas looked at them. And he thought.

'Pigeons have a marvellous sense of direction, but they couldn't pull a sleigh. Cats are good at finding places, but they're not strong enough. Dogs are strong, but they bark a lot, so they might wake the children up when I'm in the chimney. What about horses? They might do, but how could I look at my map when I'm holding the reins?'

Father Christmas stroked his long white beard.

'Well?' asked a chirpy squirrel. 'Who is going to pull that sleigh for you?'

'I just don't know,' answered Father Christmas. And then he saw two large, shadowy figures at the back of the hall.

'Oh, but I do!' he cried out, jumping to his feet. 'My friends, please come forward.'

When he pointed to them, Dasher and Dancer, the two reindeers at the back of the hall, came shyly to the front.

'Perfect,' said Father Christmas, 'just perfect. You're both very strong and I can clip my maps to your antlers. Then, when we're racing through the sky on Christmas Eve I'll know exactly where we're going.'

Dasher and Dancer pawed the ground with their feet.

'So, my friends, will you help on Christmas Eve?' went on Father Christmas.

Would they? Dasher and Dancer had never been so thrilled in their lives. From now on, every Christmas Eve, they would have one of the best jobs in the world!

Well, as I said, this all happened a long, long time ago. But … if you were very, very lucky to see a sleigh being pulled across a moonlit sky one Christmas Eve … you'd see two reindeers who were still smiling!

(Activity sheet 23 relates specifically to this story. It would probably be most effective if used immediately after the reading of the story.)

Christmas is coming

Christmas is coming,
The geese are getting fat,
Please put a penny
In the old man's hat.
If you haven't got a penny,
A ha'penny will do.
If you haven't got a ha'penny
A farthing will do
If you haven't got a farthing
Then God bless you.

Anon

The Present

(This is an adaptation of a thirteenth century Islamic story.)

Long, long ago a man and his wife lived in a very hot land. For months and months there was no rain and everything was dry and covered in dust. Every year it was like this.

One day, the man, whose name was Tariq, put his arm round his wife.

'We can't go on like this,' he said. 'Every year we are near to starving because we can't get enough water to make things grow.'

'But what can we do?' asked his wife.

'We've got to ask for help,' replied Tariq, wiping the sweat from his brow. There is a famous king who lives one week's journey from here. If I take him a present he might help us.'

'A present? But what can we give a king?'

'Ah,' whispered Tariq, nodding wisely. 'I'll take him some of the most precious things I have.'

'You don't mean...' began his wife.

'I do,' interrupted Tariq. 'I'll take him a cup of water.'

Now for all those people who lived in the bone-dry desert, water was the most precious thing they had. For Tariq to take the king a cup of water was to take the best present he could think of.

So he set off. With a cover over the cup of water to stop the dust getting into it, he walked mile after mile over the scorching hot, tiring, unfriendly desert.

Each day was the same and, by the time he reached the great city of the king, Tariq was absolutely tired out. Dragging his weary feet through the narrow streets, he reached the king's palace.

Now the palace was a magnificent building and to reach it a visitor had to go through the king's garden. Tariq went through the gate into the enormous garden – and his heart sank right down to the bottom of his sandals.

The garden was full of beautiful green lawns as far as he could see. Twisting through the lawns was a bubbling, sparkling river and dotted amongst the shining green were fountains, shooting great cascades of water up into the sky.

Water! Tariq had never seen so much of it in his life.

Water! And he had brought this great king a small cup of it as a present. Sadly he turned to go home.

'One moment, please.'

A voice spoke to him.

Turning, he saw one of the king's gardeners.

'Can I ask what you are doing in the royal gardens? Nobody is supposed to come in here without the king's permission, you know.'

'Oh, I'm very sorry,' said Tariq. 'But I was bringing him a present, you see.'

'That's different, come with me.'

So saying, the gardener led the way to a door in the garden wall.

'But you don't understand ... now I can't ... please...'

Stuttering and stammering Tariq followed the gardener, but almost before he knew what was happening he was being led along a great corridor by a servant.

Then he was shown into an enormous room. Rich curtains hung by the windows and his feet sank into a deep thick carpet. There, in front of him, sitting on a throne, was the king!

'Come forward, my friend. I hear you've brought something for me.'

At the sound of the king's voice Tariq found that he could no longer speak. This was terrible. The king would think him a complete fool. A cup of water indeed. He might even be killed for being so insulting.

Nervously he approached the king and handed over the dust-covered cup. Silently the king looked at it – and then at Tariq. He saw a man thin and tired, covered in dirt and dust, wearing poor clothes and obviously worn out.

Gently the king lifted the lid off the cup. Then he slowly raised the cup to his lips and drank every drop of water in it.

There was a long pause. Then the king spoke.

'My friend,' he said, 'that was the best cup of water I have ever drunk in my life. For one who has brought me such a wonderful present, there must be something in return.'

The king clapped his hands. A servant immediately came forward.

'Fill this cup with jewels for my friend here – and see that he gets safely home.'

The servant bowed – and Tariq just managed to stutter a whispered 'thank you' to the king.

A week later Tariq sat again with his wife in their tiny house. He had just finished telling her the fantastic story.

She smiled.

'For a man to value such a small gift that he didn't even need, and then to show such kindness – no wonder he is a great king.'

Recipe for Father Christmas

Take

A fat jolly face
And a mass of white hair
And a big cheery grin
And hold it right there.

Add

A sweeping red cloak
Two books, big and black
A head covering hood
And a toy filled sack.

Mix in	A booming loud laugh
	And a great sense of fun
	A spirit for giving
	And a job to be done.
Bake	With a large pile of letters
	And then add some more
	A sledge and two reindeers
	And chimneys galore.
Garnish with	The magic of Christmas Eve.

Oscar Reid

The Third Shepherd

Ezra looked up at the stars which studded the night sky. He was only a boy and the youngest shepherd in the group. Even though he wasn't on watch he couldn't sleep. There was just something strange about tonight. It was … he just couldn't explain it.

Below the group of shepherds even the sheep seemed restless. They were all gathered safely together in a soft grassy spot. The day's work of leading them through the rocks with the dangerous hidden snakes was over.

'Ezra, are you asleep?'

A voice whispered in the darkness. It was Eleh, another boy shepherd.

'No,' whispered Ezra. 'I can't sleep tonight.'

'Neither can I. I've tried putting my head under my abayeh but it's no good.'

'I've just got this strange feeling that something special is going to happen,' went on Ezra, 'and we should stay awake to see what it is.'

A man's loud voice suddenly boomed out from the nearby fireside.

'You two lads – get to sleep. We've got a hard day's work tomorrow and I want you both fresh for it.'

This was Ezekiel, the leader of the group. He ruled both men and sheep very firmly, but fairly too.

'And let me tell you …' went on Ezekiel.

But what it was he was going to tell them the boys never knew. Before the old man could finish speaking the night seemed to explode into briliant lights and noise.

There were cries of fear from even the toughest of the shepherds and when Ezra peered fearfully over the edge of his abayeh he could see that the light was so bright it seemed as if it night had turned into day. What happened next was at first terrifying … and then marvellous.

'Fear not,' echoed a deep, calm voice around the hillsides. The voice then went on to tell of the birth of a king in the nearby town of Bethlehem. And then, along with the brilliant light, there was this wonderful singing.

As suddenly as it began the voice and the noise, light and singing disappeared. But now the night was alive with activity.

'Right,' commanded Ezekiel. 'Some lambs – and hurry up, we must be on our way.'

'It's not every night poor shepherds can greet a new born king,' called one of the men.

'And take him lambs as a present,' muttered another.

'Ezra ... Eleh!'

The boys heard their names called. Scrambling to their feet they made their way towards the leader. What excitement – they were going down to Bethlehem in the middle of the night to see a king! At least ...

'Now you two,' said Ezekiel sternly. 'You've got an important job to do.'

Ezra's heart sank.

'But master ... you mean ... we're not ...'

All around there was hustle and bustle. Men were tightening girdles round their abayehs. Lambs were being fetched from the flock. Staffs knocked against rocks and handfuls of raisins were being chewed in the excitement. Ezekiel ignored all this.

'As I said,' he went on. 'You've got an important job to do. The men and I have to find a stable in Bethlehem and take our gifts to this new born king. Whilst we are away – and I don't know how long that will be – somebody's got to look after the sheep.'

'And that's Eleh and me,' interrupted Ezra. He just couldn't keep the disappointment out of his voice.

Minutes later, after a firm squeeze on their shoulders from Ezekiel, the two boys found themselves alone with the huge flock of sheep. Now their feelings of first excitement and then disappointment gave way to something else. They were worried. They'd never been in charge before. What if some of the sheep wandered off and got lost in a rock cleft – or were attacked by snakes ... or ... or ...

'I'm scared,' whispered Eleh.

'Don't be,' replied Ezra, more bravely than he felt. 'Let's go and check on the sheep.'

Taking their staffs in their hands the two boys moved down the hillside. When they reached the great ring of sheep they spread out – one going round one way, and the other in the opposite direction.

As he walked slowly round gently easing back the odd sheep with his staff, Ezra watched the moon slide out from behind a cloud. Away to the east lights twinkled in Bethlehem and he could almost feel the excitement and commotion that was going on there.

Then Ezra dropped his eyes and peered towards the other side of the flock to see if he could see Eleh.

'Oh yes, there he is,' he muttered to himself as he saw a shadowy figure. 'He must be ...'

He stopped muttering. He could see Eleh. But ... yes there was no mistake. Another figure was slowly circling the flock too. But ...

Ezra knew that only Eleh and he of the shepherd band had stayed behind so … who was this stranger?

Then a feeling of amazing calm and wonder came over him. True he wasn't in Bethlehem but something very special was happening out here tonight too. No sheep were going to wander off or get hurt. That was certain. This was just a wonderful place to be and a wonderful time to be alive.

Once again Ezra looked at the-sure footed figure moving slowly and gracefully round the sheep. For a moment it seemed as if the figure looked back and a hand came up in greeting.

'Thank you,' said Ezra aloud, looking up once again to the sky. 'Thank you.'

December

December is a candle
Burning through the night,
Showing the birth of Jesus
Filling the world with light.

(Composed by a group of primary children.)

The Holly Tree's Story

'Ah,' sighed the holly tree, 'if only I didn't look such an unfriendly tree. My leaves are prickly until they grow brown and die and I've got no fruit for people to come and enjoy. I wish somebody would give me the chance to show I can be as helpful as other trees.'

So thought the holly as it stood, rather lonely, a little way from all the other trees.

Then one night a cold and tired man came pushing into the wood.

'I've got to get some wood quickly! That new born baby must be kept warm during the night.'

As he was in such a hurry he headed straight for the holly tree, which was the first one to take his eye. Shouldering its prickly leaves aside, he pulled it from the ground and dragged it off behind him.

'Now to get back to that stable,' he thought.

As soon as he reached the stable he chopped branches from the holly tree and made a fire. It blazed up quickly.

All through the long night the fire warmed the stable. Whenever its flames seemed in danger of dying down a small robin flew down from the roof and fanned them with its wings. Eventually the first light of dawn appeared and the exhausted bird flew back to the roof, its breast to remain red for ever after its work over the fire.

The man and woman sat staring into what was left of the fire. The baby slept soundly.

'Joseph,' said Mary, 'that fire has been wonderful. It has kept our baby warm all night.'

'You're right,' replied the man, smiling at his wife, and poking at what remained of the glowing red embers.

So the holly tree had been given a chance to prove how it could be helpful.

From that moment onwards it became as special as the night during which Jesus was born. Its leaves remained shiny, green and bright all the year round. And the tree glows with red berries which look just like the embers which had glowed in the fire. What is more, the holly was no longer left alone and untouched in the woods. Since then it has been used to decorate homes and to remind people of that very first Christmas.

The Christmas Cat

'Yippee!'

'We're off'

'What have you got in your sandwiches?'

Class 5 of Shipton School were excited. It was the day of their Christmas outing. They were going to a Christmas puppet show at the musuem. And they were going to have a picnic there.

Slowly the coach drove out of the school gates. Miss Hope waved to Mr Bigley the caretaker as he closed the gated behind them. Soon they were on the motorway.

'Let's wave to every car that passes us,' shouted Sam, pressing his nose against the window.

'Great idea,' agreed Winston, already waving.

They'd been travelling for nearly an hour when there was a shout from the back of the coach. It was from Katrina, the tallest girl in the class.

'Miss – I feel sick.'

'Oh dear, ' grumbled Mr Marriner, the headmaster.

'Don't worry,' smiled Miss Hope. 'I'll see to it.'

Pushing back her long curly hair, the class teacher went to sit beside Katrina.

'We've turned off the motorway now,' she said kindly. 'We'll soon stop and you can have some fresh air.'

Ten minutes later the coach stopped near a little wood.

'Reckon there's any wolves in there?' grinned Winston.

The children put their coats on and ran round the edge of the wood. Miss Hope gave Katrina a drink and walked up and down with her. Mr Marriner looked at his watch.

'Right,' he shouted. 'We're late. Everybody back on the coach.'

Soon everybody was back in their seats. The driver climbed in.

'Here we go then kids,' he shouted, and turned the key to start the engine. Nothing happened. He turned the key again ... and again ... and again. Nothing happened.

They'd broken down!

Five minutes later the driver shook his head as he looked at the coach's engine.

'Big job,' he said to Mr Marriner. 'I'll use my phone to call a mechanic. But we'll be here for three hours I reckon.'

'But we should be starting back by then,' gasped Mr Marriner. 'And we're not even there yet!'

'Got a bit o' trouble?'

Mr Marriner and the driver turned to see who had spoken. It was an enormous man in a thick brown jacket and huge wellington boots. He had spiky, straw coloured hair and eyes the same colour as his jacket.

Mr Marriner told the stranger what had happened.

'That's no problem then,' boomed the man. 'My nam's Ted Vale and I've got a farm just through the woods. Let's take the children there for the afternoon. You can phone the musuems and cancel the visit. Maybe they'll like the farm just as much.'

'What a wonderful idea,' shouted Miss Hope, who had just got out of the coach.

'Well I'm not so sure ...' grumbled Mr Marriner, taking his glasses off worriedly.

'It'll be marvellous!' went on Miss Hope, clapping her hands.

'Course it will,' agreed Ted Vale.

So Class 5 bundled off the coach.

'Hear that,' said Sam. 'We're going to a farm.'

'Great,' said Kelly, 'better than a museum anyway.'

'Do you think they'll have dogs that bite?' asked Katrina nervously.

'Listen children,' called Miss Hope. 'This is Mr Vale and he's going to take us to his farm for the afternoon. Make sure you've got your packed lunches. Now get into pairs.'

'Right lads and lasses,' shouted Ted Vale, waving his stick in the air. 'Off we go. Hi-ho, hi-ho, off to the farm we go.'

Singing loudly Ted stode along a path through the woods. Class 5 followed him, towards a field of cows.

'All mine,' shouted Ted. 'Mind your feet ... hi-ho ... hi-ho...'

'What does he mean Miss? 'Watch your feet?'

'Well ...' began Miss Hope, when there was a great shout from Sam.

'Ugh ...ugh!'

'Ha, ha,' laughed Winston. 'You've stood in one.'

Sure enough Sam had stood in a large cow pat. Everybody had to wait while he cleaned his shoes on some thick grass.

'See over there,' said Ted, when they got going again. He pointed to a piece of fenced off land. It was just in front of the farm.

'That's Wild Walter in there.'

'Who's he, Mr Vale?'

'He's a billy goat,' said Ted. He's not frightened of anybody of anything. And when he gets fed up he sometimes charges through the fence and eats my flowers. Then I get angry.'

The children crowded round the fence. Wild Walter looked at them, twitching his beard and shaking his horns.

'Don't annoy him,' warned Mr Marriner worriedly.

Looking as good as gold Wild Walter wandered over to where Sam, Winston, Beth and Kelly were standing. Then, quick as a flash, he stuck his head through the fence. He grabbed the paper bag with Kelly's sandwiches in.

'Help – he's pinched my lunch!' shouted Kelly.

Wild Walter was now clomping round his patch, munching Kelly's lunch.

'He's a scoundrel,' shouted Ted.

'Don't worry,' said Miss Hope. 'We've plenty more to share with you, Kelly.'

'Come and see Pearl,' beckoned Ted.

Class 5 followed Ted. They went past geese, hens, two horses and a tractor. In one part of the farmyard a shaggy dog and a rooster stared at them.

'That's Billy,' said Ted, pointing at the dog. 'He likes children.'

'What about him?' asked Sam, pointing at the rooster.

'He's called Goliath,' said Ted, 'and he doesn't like anybody.'

Then they turned a corner and came to another pen.

'Cor,' shouted Winston.

'She's enormous,' muttered Beth.

There in the pigsty, was Pearl the pig. Scuffling round her were twelve little piglets.

'Look at their curly tails,' said Kelly.

'And their funny eyes,' whispered Katrina.

'Aah,' said Ted. 'Pigs are not as daft as they look you know. But one thing you can be sure about – they are always hungry!'

'Hello everybody.'

The children turned round to see who had spoken to them. Behind them stood a lady with grey hair twisted into a bun. Kind eyes looked at them through big glasses. But somehow she looked sad.

Ted went and put his arm round her.

'This is Mrs Vale, everybody – but I've got to tell you, she's not very happy at the moment.'

'No,' said Mrs Vale. 'You see it's our cat, Prudence. She was my Christmas present last year. She's lovely and ... she's just ... disappeared.'

'Been gone nearly two days' said Ted.

'Do you think she's trapped somewhere?' asked Miss Hope.

'That's what I worry about, dear,' sighed Mrs Vale.

Just then a large raindrop landed on Sam's head.

'It's raining,' he shouted.

Then the rain started to pour down.

'Come on everybody,' called Mrs Vale. 'Ted, get them all in the barn while I get some drinks.'

Everybody ran through the rain into a huge barn.

Ten minutes later Class 5 were eating their sandwiches. Mrs Vale brought a big tray of hot drinks.

'Winston,' whispered Sam.

'Yeah.'

'Why don't we creep off while nobody's looking. There's a ladder back there. We can climb up it and explore.'

Sam and Winston crept to the back of the barn. Nobody was looking. They reached the ladder and quickly climbed up.

'It's great up here,' whispered Sam.

Winston nodded. The two boys were on a big platform with bundles of straw piled on it.

'Now let's explore,' hissed Winston.

Meanwhile, down below, Mr Marriner was looking at his watch.

'It's time we were getting back to the coach, Miss Hope,' he said.

'Right Mr Marriner, but first we must say a big thank you to Mr and Mrs Vale.'

Miss Hope stood up, pushed back her long curly hair, and clapped her hands.

'Listen, children. It's stopped raining and its time for us to get back to the coach now. But before that we've got to thank Mr and Mrs Vale for giving us such a wonderful time. Let's do that by giving then a great big clap.'

For what seemed ages Class 5 clapped and cheered. Ted put his arm round MrsVale and gave one of his big smiles.

'We've loved having you here,' said Mrs Vale kindly.

'Now,' said Mr Marriner, 'into pairs please.'

'Miss ... Miss ...,' stuttered Katrina. 'It's Sam and Winston. They're not here!'

'What!' snapped Mr Marriner. 'Where...'

Just then there was a great shout.

'We've found her!'

Winston and Sam appeared on the platform at the top of the ladder. In Sam's arms was – Prudence the cat!

Everybody went mad again. Class 5 started cheering and clapping, Mrs Vale burst into tears and Ted raced up the ladder like a ten year old. When he and Sam, Winston and Prudence were back on the ground everybody crowded round.

'We thought we heard something,' said Winston.

'And then we found her,'said Sam. 'Trapped between two bales of straw.'

'You shouldn't have ...' began Mr Marriner, but Miss Hope interrupted.

'You've made Mrs Vale happy again boys,' she said.

'Aye – they have that,' agreed Ted.

'Prudence is back,' sighed Mrs Vale. 'She's this year's Christmas present all over again. Thank you boys.'

Suddenly everybody started cheering again. What a day it had been!

I Saw Three Ships

I saw three ships come sailing in,
On Christmas day, on Christmas day,
I saw three ships come sailing in,
On Christmas day in the morning.

And what was in those ships all three?
On Christmas day, on Christmas day,
And what was in those ships all three?
On Christmas day in the morning.

Our Saviour Christ and his lady,
On Christmas day, on Christmas day,
Our Saviour Christ and his lady,
On Christmas day in the morning.

Pray, whither sailed those ships all three?
On Christmas day, on Christmas day,
Pray, whither sailed those ships all three?
On Christmas day in the morning.

O, they sailed into Bethlehem,
On Christmas day, on Christmas day
O, they sailed into Bethlehem,
On Christmas day in the morning.

Traditional

My gran says...

Have you ever asked your gran what Christmas was like when she was a little girl? I have. This is what she said.

'When I was a little girl we lived in a small village. All the men in the village worked in a coal mine and they only got one day's holiday at Christmas. So you can see why Christmas day was very special.

My sisters and I helped Mum do the cooking. We made mince pies and a very big Christmas cake. We made a Christmas pudding and we all stirred it. We also put silver threepenny bits in the pudding.

We kept all the food in a big cupboard in the larder. We had no fridge. This didn't matter because the house was very cold. We only had one fire, in the room where we ate our meals.

But then, on Christmas Eve, Mum lit the fire in the front room. We never went in there usually. But this was a very special time. We hung paper chains from one corner of the room to the other. We put up our little Christmas tree. It came down from the loft once a year.

We hung little toys and chocolates on the Christmas tree. Then mum draped it with twinkling lights. When we'd done all this it was nearly time to go to bed. But we waited for Dad to come from work first.

When he came in he was dirty from the coal mine. He took off his big boots and got washed in front of the fire. Then he took my two sisters and me on his knee. My brother sat on the floor beside us.

'Now,' said Dad in his deep voice. 'Sent all your letters off to Father Christmas?'

'Yes Dad.'

'Hope you didn't ask for too much.'

'No Dad.'

'Well I hope he brings you just want you want. Now off to bed.'

Then we kissed Dad and Mum and went up to our bedroom. We girls all slept in the same bedroom. My brother slept with my grandad.

When we got to the bedroom we hung up our stockings. Mine was a red and white hooped stocking. It was just like the ones the Sunderland footballers wore. Each stocking hung off the end of the big double bed.

'Wonder what time he'll come?' whispered my sister Ada.

'It's always midnight,' chirped Lily, the oldest. 'Don't you know anything?'

We always decided that we would stay awake. Then we would see Father Christmas coming into the bedroom and filling our stockings. But, no matter how hard we tried we just couldn't stay awake.

Lily was always the first one up on Christmas morning.

'He's been!' she would cry, when it was still early, dark and cold. 'He's been!'

In a flash we were all up. Looking through our stockings was the most magical of magic moments. Little dolls, stamps, a book, a comic, some sweets, an apple. All were pulled out with an unimaginable thrill. Yes, Christmas was a really wonderful time!

'Janet'

Chrisimus Day

There was a pig went out to dig,
Chrisimus day, Chrisimus day,
There was a pig went out to dig
On Chrisimus day in the morning.

There was a cow went out to plough,
Chrisimus day, Chrisimus day,
There was a cow went out to plough
On Chrisimus day in the morning.

There was a sparrow went out to harrow,
Chrisimus day, Chrisimus day,
There was a sparrow went out to harrow,
On Chrisimus day in the morning.

There was a drake went out to rake,
Chrisimus day, Chrisimus day,
There was a drake went out to rake,
On Chrisimus day in the morning.

There was a crow went out to sow,
Chrisimus day, Chrisimus day,
There was a crow went out to sow
On Chrisimus day in the morning.

There was a sheep went out to reap,
Chrisimus day, Chrisimus day,
There was a sheep went out to reap
On Chrisimus day in the morning.

(Anon)

Assemblies for Christmas

6

(Activity sheets 24 – 25)

One of the items which gives teachers particular food for thought is the appearance of the inoffensive little 'who's taking assembly?' list – especially at Christmas. Apart from the grander productions December still requires many assemblies, and these are often presented by classes rather than an individual.

Some practical assemblies are suggested after these notes but there are some important general comments which apply to all of them.

Ralph R. Upton is not a name which claims instant recognition. In the early part of the twentieth century Mr Upton devised a sign to be displayed at all American railway crossings. It simply said: 'Stop – Look – Listen!' If we add two more words to this, namely: 'Think – Do;' we have a phrase which does much to encompass the spirit of Christmas and helps to focus on the requirements of class assemblies.

When preparing a class assembly a consideration of resources is vital. This consideration might include:

1 Music – for entry, background, sound effects and atmosphere.
2 Carols – what is available, what is known by the class and/or the whole school.
3 Any other sounds required for background effects.
4 Written material – for information, inspiration, and reading aloud.
5 Materials – paint, paper, photographs, objects, etc. for visual effects.
6 Physical resources of the hall – stage, blocks, benches, seating arrangements etc. so that the presentation can make the fullest use of them, and the seating arrangements ensure that the audience can see and hear well.

Of equal importance are the human resources. Considerations here might include:

1 Other adults to be involved – is a pianist available for accompaniment? Are there props or sound effects which require supervision by another teacher, welfare assistant or parent? Is there to be a guest speaker, video operator? etc.
2 Using the strengths of the children – who are best at doing preparatory work beforehand? Who are the best readers, singers, actors, mimer? Who are the most reliable with regard to musical accompaniments, operation of any equipment? etc.

Once all of these thing have been considered then a 'theme' for the presentation might be the next step. Many Christmas themes – gifts, promises, birth, journeys, homes, families etc. are very familiar. There exists such a wealth of material to choose from however that originality and verve can be brought to each.

Indeed there seems only one final warning to heed: 'One problem is the rescue the truth of Christmas from the commercial jungle, without preaching and without thwarting the festal impulse.' (Denys Thompson)

On a practical note, some of the assemblies which follow contain passages for choral speaking by the presenting class. In order to make the arranging of this easier for the teacher these choral passages are reproduced on Activity Sheet 24.

Assembly 1: 'What are you giving for Christmas?'

This assembly could begin by having a normal situation reversed. Instead of having the audience in the hall waiting for the presenters to begin, or make a dramatic entry, the presenting class is in place first. They sing some well known carols as the other children join them in the hall.

At the entrance to the hall some simple placards inviting the audience to join in immediately with the singing would hopefully engender a feeling of everybody enjoying the singing together. This 'sharing' theme is an important one for this assembly.

Once everyone is in the hall the carol singing ends and one of the presenting children speaks.

SPEAKER 1: 'Good morning, everybody, (Wait for response.) 'We have been doing some maths work in our class. Look ...'

At this stage several of the other children come forward with large cut-out shapes – squares, rectangles, triangles, circles. (Activity Sheets 3 and 4 could be used here too.) Once they have shown these shapes to the audience a second speaker could elicit a response from the gathering.

SPEAKER 2: 'Can you tell us what these shapes are called? Please put up your hands to answer.'

There will obviously be some interplay at this stage between Speaker 2 and the audience, and the names of the shapes will be established. The assembly then continues with a third speaker.

SPEAKER 3: 'Yes, we all do maths in this school. We have already learned a lot about shapes.'

A series of other speakers (well prepared and rehearsed) then take up the progression.

SPEAKER 4: 'But we know about a little boy who was fantastic at maths.'

SPEAKER 5: 'His name was Zerah. When he was six years old he was better at maths than any teacher.'

SPEAKER 4: 'He was given a special test.'

SPEAKER 5: 'A very clever teacher said to him – 'How many minutes are there in 48 years?'

SPEAKER 4: 'Without writing anything down Zerah answered!'

SPEAKER 5: ''25 million, 228 thousand, 800,' he said.'

SPEAKER 4: 'He was right.'

At this point in the assembly a brief piece of choral speaking by the presenting group adds impact. The class could say:

'Yes. Zerah had a great gift. But lots of people in our class have gifts too. Look.'

This piece of choral speaking provides the introduction for various members of the group to illustrate their 'gifts'. Pre-assembly work will have been done on this and a selection from as wide a range as possible would be the most effective. Thus the assembly might now contain a recorder player in action, some children who are good at PE giving some examples of their skill, gifted artists showing some of their work – and so on. There is always scope for the unusual here too – somebody who is really good at mime, or who can whistle, or tap dance, or say something in another language. The whole point of this part of the service is that it enables the presenting class to share some of their 'gifts' with the school as a whole.

Once this presentation is over then progress could be made towards stimulating thought on a wider scale. Following the various activities this could again be done by the return of the speakers.

SPEAKER 1: 'We have seen that gifts give great pleasure when they are shared.'

SPEAKER 2: 'What gifts can we all share at Christmas?'

At this stage various members of the group could step out and make comments like the following, or alternatively this might be done as some more choral work.

'We could share smiles. A smile makes everybody feel better.'

'We could share energy. We could help our mums and dads and people who are older or not well.'

'We could share words. Words like 'please' and 'thank you' – and show we always mean them!'

'We could share being friends with other children who are not usually our special friends!'

There is scope for many more comments here which might be appropriate to a particular group of children or school. When this session is over the choral speakers might make another comment:

'Dear God,

This Christmas help us to share our gifts as much as we can.
Help us to be kind and thoughtful, polite and helpful. Amen.

(*These phrases are reproduced on Activity Sheet 24.*)

At this point the assembly could be concluded by a final prayer. This might be read, or spoken, by the teacher. One suggestion is:

'This morning we have thought about gifts – giving and sharing.
So often people say to us: 'What are you getting for Christmas?'
This morning might have made us think : 'What are you giving for Christmas?'

Information for the teacher

The resources for this assembly could well have come up naturally in maths work on shapes – or via the relevant activity sheets in this book.

The 'gifts' displayed by the children will of course depend upon the skills available.

It might be useful for the teacher to have some more information about Zerah, the boy mathematical genius. Zerah Coburn was born in America in 1804 and was found to be a genius at maths by the time he was six years old. He was brought to England at eight and 'the very clever teacher' referred to in the text was in fact a panel of the best scholars and teachers who gathered together to test the boy. He solved the question about the number of minutes in 48 years in a matter of seconds – doing the sum involving years, leap years, months, weeks, days, hours and minutes without recourse to anything but his mental ability.

Assembly 2: Christmas Peace

This assembly could begin with all of the audience gathered in the hall first. While they are assembling, a piece of really tranquil, sleepy music could be played on the sound system (or by a pianist if one is available). When everyone is in place the presenting class enters. Nine of the children of this group carry a large card each. On these nine cards, written as large as possible are the letters: SMASHTRIC. The audience should not be able to see these letters at first.

Once the presenters are in position the tranquil music could stop and they could issue a choral 'Good morning everybody' to the audience. Once the reply has been received there could be a short pause and then, at a given signal from the teacher the whole group could shout together:

'COCK – A – DOODLE – DOO!'

Obviously this will make an impact on the audience. When they have settled down a series of speakers gets the assembly further under way.

SPEAKER 1: 'The cock is the creature which calls out his message when a new day is about to start.'

SPEAKER 2: 'New days are very busy now ...'

SPEAKER 3: 'We have to get up to go to school.'

SPEAKER 4: 'Our dads and mums have to go to work.'

SPEAKER 1: 'There is lots of traffic everywhere.'

SPEAKER 2: 'Cars, buses and lorries are stuck in traffic jams.'

SPEAKER 3: 'Trains are full of people.'

SPEAKER 4: 'Everybody is busy ... busy ... busy.'

As Speaker 4 intones more and more 'busys' the whole class could join in with him/her building up a rhythm of 'busy ...busy ...busy.' Then Speaker 1 claps his or her hands and, once silence has been re-established, speaks again.

SPEAKER 1: 'When the world is in such a rush ...'

SPEAKER 2: 'People often forget their manners ...'

SPEAKER 3: They argue with each other ...'

SPEAKER 4: 'Mistakes are made ...'

SPEAKER 1: 'It gets a bit like this ...'

At this point the nine children bearing the cards (having practised thoroughly beforehand!) push and jostle each other in a bad-tempered way.

They call out … 'We've got a message for you' …as they do so.

Finally after apparent chaos they reveal their letters in the following sequence to make up the non-word SMASHTRIC.

There could be another quite lengthy pause here – to emphasise the point that no-one knows quite what to make of this. Then, while the audience are still looking, the presenting class again, at an appropriate signal from the teacher, calls out another sustained …

COCK – A – DOODLE – DOO … COCK – A – DOODLE – DOO …

After about six of these the teacher holds up her hand and steps out to the front. She says:

'Did you know that there was one time when the cock is supposed to have crowed right through the night? He did this to make sure everyone got rid of all their selfish thoughts and bad tempers. He did this right through the very first Christmas Eve – just before Jesus was born. And so on that first, very special Christmas day all the hustle and bustle and noise and arguments stopped for that wonderful peaceful time.'

As the teacher is saying this the children holding the cards re-arrange themselves (or be re-arranged) so that their sequence of letters now spell out: CHRISTMAS.

The teacher's comment and the letter re-arrangement would aim to be completed as near to simultaneously as possible and as soon as this is so both presenters and audience sing a carol. In view of the reference so far 'Silent Night' would be a good choice if the children know it.

Once this singing is finished the teacher speaks again:

'That first Christmas gave us a time which we still feel is very special. A time when we try to think of others, to be kind and thoughtful and gentle. A famous man once said: 'There seems a magic in the very name of Christmas. Bad tempers, jealousy and arguments are forgotten … I wish it was Christmas the whole year through.'

At this point one of the child speakers could step forward again:

SPEAKER1:   'We are going to finish our service today with a beautiful Christmas poem.'

This poem could be spoken by all the class in choral form. It is:

> Winds through the olive trees
> Softly did blow,
> Round little Bethlehem
> Long, long ago.
>
> Sheep on the hillside lay
> Whiter than snow;
> Shepherds were watching them,
> Long, long ago.

Then from the happy sky,
Angels bent low,
Singing their songs of joy,
Long, long ago.

For in a manger bed,
Cradled we know,
Christ came to Bethlehem
Long, long ago.

(Anon)

(This poem is also reproduced on Activity Sheet 25.)

Information for the teacher

Some of the references here have been adapted to make them more suitable for use with young children.

1 An old legend maintained that the cock crowed all night on Christmas Eve to keep away evil from the following day.

2 'A famous man once said…': the famous man was in fact Dickens and the quotation which has been adapted here come from *Sketches by Boz*. It actually reads: 'There seems a magic in the very name of Christmas. Jealousies and arguments are forgotten … would that Christmas lasted the whole year through.'

3 A particularly appropriate carol, in both words and music, for use with this service is Jancis Harvey's smooth and flowing 'Little Star'. One source for it is the BBC's *Come and Praise* Vol. 2.

Assembly 3: A Time of Journeys

This assembly might begin with no background music, in order to heighten the evocative effect of the introductory music when it is used. Following the audience gathering in the hall, the presenting class could then enter and take up their places.

At this stage a piece of music creating a sense of travel or a journey could be played. Teachers will have their own ideas of what is suitable here and those with long memories and/or old recordings will have an even wider choice of material. 'The Flying Dutchman Overture' by Wagner portrays a rough sea voyage very well; 'Coronation Scot' and 'Chatanooga Choo Choo' are varied but excellent 'train' themes. One other tune that has an interesting anecdote attached to it is 'Sentimental Journey'. Many recordings were made of this song (Doris Day, Ella Fitzgerald, Duke Ellington etc.) and it is not too difficult to find. During the Second World War when ships containing US servicemen going abroad passed under San Francisco's Golden Gate Bridge this tune was played on the ship's PA system to re-inforce troops' morale in that their 'journeys' would ultimately lead them home.

After the playing of the 'travel/journey' introductory music the teacher might make some reference to it, and to the fact that this morning's assembly is about journeys. The action moves on to a mimed presentation of the journey made by Mary and Joseph. As this action is taking place a commentary is read out which links with the drama taking place:

Long, long ago a couple called Mary and Joseph lived in Nazareth. One day Joseph came home. He was very worried.

'What's the matter, Joseph?' asked Mary.

'We've got to go on a journey to Bethlehem,' he replied.

'Why?' gasped Mary.

'The Roman Emperor says everybody has to go back to where they were born. This is so he can make us all pay taxes.'

'But Joseph,' went on Mary, 'I'm going to have a baby and it's such a long way to Bethlehem.'

'I know, my dear, but it's got to be done.'

So Joseph and Mary set off on their long journey. Mary rode on a donkey and Joseph walked in front leading them. They travelled over high rough ground. At night Joseph wrapped his thick coat of sheep's wool round his wife to keep her warm.

As they travelled they met more and more people. They were all going to Bethlehem too. This made Joseph worry.

'When we get there it's going to be terribly crowded,' he thought. 'I wonder if I'll be able to find anywhere for Mary to stay.'

Then, as the sun was going down one afternoon, they saw Bethlehem ahead of them. It was high on a hill. All around the hill were people camping. The smoke of camp fires drifted slowly into the air.

Soon Mary and Joseph were passing through the city gates into the crowded streets. People were pushing and shoving everywhere. There were soldiers, men, women, children, young and old. The shouts of traders rang through the streets. If you'd wanted to you could buy anything from sweets to goats.

'I'm so tired, Joseph,' Mary said.

'I know, my dear,' replied Joseph. 'We'll find somewhere soon.'

But he wasn't sure they would. All around them were other people who looked tired and miserable. He kept hearing different voices all saying the same thing.

'There's just nowhere to stay. Everywhere is full.'

At this point in the assembly the mime and commentary could be brought to a conclusion by a speaker stepping forward and saying:

SPEAKER 1:   'We now know that Joseph and Mary did find somewhere to stay, and Jesus was born that night.'

At this point in the service everyone could join in the singing of an appropriate carol. Again choice, availability and personal preference would determine what was sung here. 'Little Donkey' or 'O Little Town Of Bethlehem' are two which are particularly relevant.

Once the carol singing is ended the assembly could be taken forward by another series of speakers.

SPEAKER 1:   'Christmas is still a time of journeys.'

SPEAKER 2:   'People travel from all over the country to be with their families.'

SPEAKER 3: 'Some travel from all over the world.'

At this stage various members of the class would relate some personal anecdotes of journeys they have known at Christmas. These would have been well researched and rehearsed beforehand. They often yield some quite poignant tales. Visits from grans, grandads, aunts, uncles, cousins etc. will be raised and easy to come by. Others may be more dramatic, like this seven year old's account of going to meet her brother from Heathrow Airport.

'It was Christmas Eve. My mum said we had to go to Heathrow to pick up my brother. He lives in Australia and I hadn't seen him for ages and ages. When we got up it was dark and cold. We parked the car in a big, gloomy car park and went into the airport.

The first thing I saw was my uncle. He had been waiting so long he had fallen asleep. We all had a drink. Then we looked at a flashing sign. Beside the number of my brother's plane it flashed 'landed'.

Then we saw him. It was great. He was home for Christmas.'

When this part of the assembly is finished, affairs could be concluded with some prayers read by the teacher.

> 'Dear God, as Christmas approaches let us pray this morning for all those people who have journeys to make at this time of the year. Whether their journeys be short or long keep them safe so that they may enjoy Christmas with their families. Amen.

Information for the teacher

1   As an alternative to songs about travel an introduction of 'travel sound effects' would be equally evocative. The BBC was an excellent source of material like this and schools may have examples to hand.

   Alternatively it could be quite a diverting little pre-assembly exercise for the children to invent and create some travel sounds themselves. These could then be put on a tape for use in the assembly.

2   For those teachers who might want to refer to Biblical references for Mary and Joseph's journey then the following are relevant:

   Luke 1, vv. 26-36 – news of the impending birth.

   Luke 2, vv. 1-6 – news of the census

   Luke 2, vv. 3-5 – the journey

   Luke 2, vv. 6-7 – arrival in Bethlehem

Assembly 4: A Colourful Occasion

Many assemblies at this time of the year take place on very gloomy December days. This assembly could begin by capitalising on this. Both audience and presenting class come into the hall without any lights on and with the curtains at least part drawn.

This will create a rather sombre, dim atmosphere, which could be further intensified by the playing of a rather sad piece of introductory music. Again there is a wide range of choice but something in a minor key would be particularly suitable.

Once this rather gloomy atmosphere has had its effect, a sudden change is effected by all the lights being switched on and the curtains drawn at a carefully pre-arranged moment. At the same time, if there are stage lights available in the hall, they are switched on to give as much brilliant light as possible. As the sudden transition to light takes place the music could be changed to match it and a particularly vigorous carol could be played – 'O Come All Ye Faithful' perhaps.

After this 'darkness to light' impact has been made the assembly could progress via some short statements from a series of speakers.

SPEAKER 1: 'Christmas is a time of light and lights.'

SPEAKER 2: 'But it is a time of other colours too.'

SPEAKER 3: 'Let us look at some of them.'

When the last statement has been made two of the presenting children could unroll a large sheet of paper which has been painted red.

SPEAKER 4: 'Red is one of our favourite colours. Did you know that when a Chinese girl gets married she wears something red because it is the colour of happiness? In Russia the word for red means beautiful. Red at Christmas reminds us of Santa Claus' robes.'

When this little scene is completed two more children unfurl a sheet of blue paper:

SPEAKER 5: 'Blue is our favourite colour. Blue is the colour that stands for the sky and the sea. It also stands for being a good and faithful friend – and is the colour which means hope.'

The next unfurling is of green:

SPEAKER 6: 'Green is our favourite colour. Green is the colour of being children, of growing and and of nature. Christmas is a wonderful time for children, so green is a very important colour at this time of the year.'

The next colour to be shown is a bright, golden yellow.

SPEAKER 7: 'Golden yellow is our favourite colour. Gold stands for the glory of God who made all things. As children we all try to be 'as good as gold'. At Christmas time we especially remember a golden rule – treat everybody else as you would like them to treat you.'

At this stage the teacher intervenes to move things on to the next focal point. She directs the holders of the coloured papers to move together where all could see them. She then says something like the following:

TEACHER: 'We have heard about some of the children's favourite colours. Think about some of the words we heard in connection with these colours. Here are some reminders for you.'

At this point, having been prepared and organised beforehand, a group of children carrying words written as large as possible on pieces of card move alongside the colours and shout their words. These could include:

Happiness	Beauty	Faith	
Hope	Children	Good	Others

The teacher continues.

'All these are words which are important at Christmas. Bow your heads and listen to the following prayer.

> Dear God, Thank you for the colours of Christmas. When we see them let us think of the things they stand for. Let us pray that there is happiness in every home; beauty in the sights and sounds of Christmas; faith and hope for the coming year; care and concern for the good of children and all people everywhere. Amen.'

The service is concluded by some singing. In place of a carol (and to supplement one) that particularly appropriate hymn 'Who Put the Colours in the Rainbow' (*Come and Praise* Vol. 1, BBC) might be sung here.

Information for the teacher

1 This service would be enhanced if various artefacts showing colours could be used as background to the proceedings. Things like coloured robes, streamers, sprigs of holly and evergreens, baubles for the Christmas tree etc. would all heighten the visual aspect of the occasion.

2 More could be made of 'the golden rule' either in follow up work or in the actual assembly itself. 'Treat other people as you wish to treat them' has its source in Luke 6, verse 31.

3 As an alternative to 'O Come All Ye Faithful' as the music to emphasise the tranistion from darkness to light at the beginning of this service, then 'Candle in the Window' is a good choice. It is very lively, but very easy to play and sing. The words are reasonable for infant use. It can be found in the Christmas section of *Come and Praise* Vol. 2, (BBC).

Assembly 5: Christingle

It is quite possible that some of the children in the school will have attended a Christingle service, for these are becoming increasingly popular in parish churches throughout the country. An adaptation of such a service however makes for a very worthwhile assembly and various other useful facets can be introduced as well.

The service begins with the presenting class singing a carol. It would be advantageous if the rest of the school could join in too, and a most appropriate choice here would be 'Candle in the Window' (*Come and Praise*, Vol.2, BBC).

Following the singing of this carol the assembly begins with the presenting class showing some pictures. These could be either the children's own drawings, or photographs or illustrations of a donkey, a camel, a cat, a robin, and a sheep. As the pictures are held up the teacher could say:

TEACHER: 'Did you know that all these creatures have a special connection with Christmas? Listen carefully and you will learn something about them.'

At this point the child holding the picture of the donkey steps forward, and be joined by an 'information reader'.

READER 1: 'The donkey was very important on that first Christmas. It carried Mary on the long journey from Nazareth to Bethlehem.'

Next come the two children representing the camel.

READER 2: 'The camel too was important on that first Christmas. It was three camels who carried the three wise men who came to give their gifts to Jesus.'

The next two children could focus attention on the cat.

READER 3: 'Did you know that there was a cat in the stable when Jesus was born? Did you know that on that very same night, in the stable, she gave birth to some kittens?'

The robin is the subject of the next two children.

READER 4: 'Nobody worked harder on the night Jesus was born than the robin. As the flames of the fire got low through the long night, the robin flew down and fanned them up again. As a result his breast got redder and redder and has stayed that way ever since.'

Finally two children could focus attention on the sheep.

READER 5: 'The first ever present Jesus received was the lamb, brought by the shepherds. So they too were very special on that very special night.'

At this point the teacher takes over again. She might say:

TEACHER: 'We know Christmas is about people caring for each other. We have now heard how some animals cared for people on that very first Christmas long, long ago. People and animals go together to make up the world.'

When this point is reached there is an apparently spontaneous, but really a pre-planned and prepared interruption. When the word 'world' is reached a child could push through the ranks of the presenting class, go up to the teacher and give her an orange. The child might then say: 'This orange could represent the world'.

Two more children could then come to the front. One could be carrying a jar of raisins, the other a jar of nuts. They could then speak together.

SPEAKERS: 'There are people and animals in the world. There are also flowers and trees, crops and vegetables and fruit. These nuts and raisins represent the fruit of the world.'

Quickly following this could be four children, each bearing a picture of one of the seasons – spring, summer, autumn, winter. One of them could say:

SPEAKER: 'In the British Isles our world is made up of four seasons – spring, summer, autumn and winter.'

The teacher now takes over again.

TEACHER: 'This morning we have heard lots of interesting things. For instance we started our service by singing about a candle. So ...'

Here the teacher could take a candle which she has to hand, and light it. It could then be placed in a suitable container on the floor. She then goes on:

TEACHER: 'When we think of Christmas we think of candles, lighting up the world. And all that we have in that world. This orange represents it and all the people and animals in it.'

Christingle orange

The orange could then be placed on the floor beside the candle.

TEACHER: 'Next we heard about the fruits of the world. Now I'm going to ask our two friends to put the jars of raisins and nuts on the floor beside the orange.'

When this has been done the teacher produces four cocktail sticks and explains how each of these could represent a season of the year. They could then be laid on the floor beside the other objects. The teacher then produces a red ribbon and holds it up for everyone to see. She could then say …

TEACHER: 'And now here is something red – a colour we all think of at Christmas time. If I put it on the floor too you will see we have … a candle, an orange, four cocktail sticks, some nuts and raisins and a red ribbon. Now if we put all three together we would get something which reminds us of everything we have been talking about this morning.'

At this point another adult could appear with a previously prepared, and complete, Christingle. This is given to the presenting teacher who holds it up for everybody to see. The service could then be concluded with the following choral prayer:

> 'Let us think this Christmas of our world, and all the living things in it. Let us especially give thanks for our families at this very special time of the year. Amen.'

Proceedings are rounded off with everybody singing a final carol. A good choice here might be the cheerful and rhythmic 'Mary Had a Baby'. Already well known to many Key Stage 1 children it too can be found in *Come and Praise* Vol. 2.

Information for the teacher

1 Traditionally the Christingle ceremony was founded in the Moravian church and the services always took place on Christmas Eve.

2 'Animals at Christmas' is a subject which could be developed and linked to a 'caring' theme in which the children could consider the long-term needs of those many animals who are given as presents at Christmas time.

3 This is one of those assemblies where any priests who have connections with the school could be invited to make a contribution.

Christmas Drama

Christmas drama with Key Stage 1 children is anything but the simple presentation the end product often appears to be. In the planning stage teachers are usually faced with several dilemmas: how do they combine original material with the 'traditional' values? Do they use written texts and if so are these available or suitable? Is it possible to 'build up' some drama by starting with discussion and exploration in the classroom?

This chapter seeks to provide some suggestions in these areas. First of all a list of 'starting points' give a base from which ideas, discussion and ultimately a mime/drama presentation might be developed.

Starters

Starter 1
Get out the class's 'dressing up' box again. Look at the clothes in there. Dress several children up. What sort of people do they look like? How might these people spend Christmas? Can we see how and what they do and say at Christmas? Can we make up a story about them?

Starter 2
You are at a bus stop waiting for the bus. On the other side of the road a house has its curtains apart and you can see inside. It is Christmas Eve and there is a tree, streamers etc. to be seen. Then the family come in. They look sad, the children are crying. Why is this? What has happened? What do you do? Develop a story from here.

Starter 3
It was Charles Lamb (1775 -1834) who gave us a quotation with which it is difficult to quibble! 'Not many sounds in life, and I include all urban and rural sounds, exceed in interest a knock at the door.'

There are many possibilities starting from this. A family are enjoying themselves one Christmas morning when there is a knock on the door. There on the threshold are a group of spacemen whose craft has crashed nearby. They are lonely, stranded, don't know what Christmas is and don't speak any recognisable language … what happens?

Another 'knock' could precede the delivery of a letter or parcel. Who is it from? Is somebody special coming? Is it an invitation to go somewhere? What effect does it have on the family? Who does what … when … how?

The final knock might be that which takes us back in time to the original story. There at the door is a man who is asking if his wife can be found a room for the night because …

Starter 4
Very simple interviews can often be used to build an effective Christmas presentation. These can be linked with traditional sources in interviews with a shepherd boy, a Magi's servant, a girl at the Inn, a Roman soldiers's daughter, the boy who looked after Mary's donkey etc.

Alternatively the children could represent modern characters whose lives are affected by Christmas – a priest, a nurse in a busy children's ward, a postman, a train driver, a boy, a girl, a teacher, a parent, a grandparent etc.

Starter 5
The idea is to present the end of a mime or drama first and then ask the question 'How did this happen?' – and then go back to the events which led up to this denouement.

An example might be to have as the first scene a silent tableau of Baboushka standing in the empty stable. A narrator could describe why she is there, and the story could then go back and start from the beginning.

Starter 6

This is the opposite approach to Starter 5 whereby some simple scenes lead up to a situation where the audience are asked 'What happens next?' From an early age children are becoming increasingly familiar with this format via the 'choice' on video programmes and 'Quest' type illustrated books.

Within a Christmas drama framework one possible development might be the story of a group of carol singers. They do well and collect some money – what do they do with it? The possibilities could be dramatically explored – spend it on themselves, their parents, the old lady who lives next door etc.?

Starter 7

For this suggestion Bible sources related to the first Christmas might be adapted and illuminated for display. They could then be read by a narrator whilst a mime of the various scenes take place to complement them. Sources might include: Joseph and Mary: Luke 1, 26-36; The census: Luke 2, 1-6; The journey: Luke 2, 3-5; No room at the inn: Luke 2, 6-7; Birth of Jesus: Luke 2,7; The shepherds: Luke, 8-18; The star: Matthew 2, 10-12; The Magi: Matthew 2, 10-12.

Starter 8

Ideas here might be originated and developed by a word, phrase or sentence – used in the context of Christmas, e.g.:

'It was the biggest surprise of my life.'

'I only borrowed it but ...' (Father Christmas's sledge, a Christmas tree, a dressing up costume, sister's favourite doll etc.).

'There's someone coming up the path.'

'We all sat down for Christmas dinner when ...'

'At last!'

'Look out!'

'Thank you.'

Drama presentations

For some schools more precise and detailed material for their Christmas presentation is welcomed. The suggestions which follow in this part of the chapter seek to meet this need, although once again their framework means that adaptation and flexibility is very easy.

1 Ben's Christmas (see 'Ben's letter' in Chapter 3)

This could be produced as a straightforward dramatic interpretation of events at the first Christmas. The framework described here allows for easy and attractive complementary music and simple but effective props.

With regard to the latter the action takes place in two locations – outside the inn and in the stable. A simple backdrop could be created:

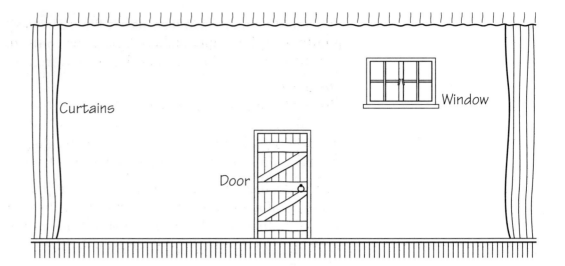

Some stage blocks could be used to elevate 'Ben' behind the scenes so that he looks through the window in both scenes.

Scene 1: all the action takes place in the doorway with Ben looking through the windows. This is the front of the inn.

Scene 2: the only required addition (after curtains have been drawn at the end of Scene 1) is a crib in the foreground. All the visitors arrive via the door and come into the foreground. Ben again is in the window.

Music: Four carols are very well suited to the actions here. All can be found in *Come and Praise Vol 2*, BBC publications. They are: 'Rise Up Shepherds', 'I Want to See Your Baby Boy', 'Mary Had a Baby', 'Little Star'.

Characters
Ben – son of the landlord of the inn

His father

Joseph

Mary

Roman soldier

'Crowd' of about six people

At least four shepherds

Three kings

Child servant of the kings

Action
Scene 1: The curtains open revealing an empty set. The 'crowd' enters from one side of the stage. They mill about in front of the inn. Ben appears at the window and looks out.

1ST PERSON IN CROWD: 'I've never known anywhere so crowded.'

2ND PERSON: 'Fancy the Romans making us all come here.'

3RD PERSON: 'I'm tired.'

4TH PERSON: 'I'm hungry.'

(Enter Roman soldier.)

ROMAN SOLDIER: 'Come on, you lot – move along.

1ST PERSON:	'But where are we going to spend the night?'
ROMAN SOLDIER:	'That's your problem.'
2ND PERSON:	'But we can't find anywhere to sleep.'
3RD PERSON:	'All the inns are full.'
4TH PERSON:	'And it's freezing camping in the hills.'
ROMAN SOLDIER:	'Move on will you. I can't help it.'

Roman soldier ushers crowd off other side of stage.

BEN:	'What a night! I've never known Bethlehem so busy. I can't even get to sleep.'

Ben peers out of the window to left of stage.

BEN:	'Oh no, here's somebody else coming. And I'm sure they're going to knock on our door. Dad will be pleased!'

Enter Joseph supporting a tired Mary. He knocks on the inn door.

LANDLORD *(from within)*:	'Go away, whoever you are!'

Joseph knocks again.

LANDLORD:	'Go away, will you!'
BEN:	'I knew he wouldn't be very happy.'

Joseph knocks again. Door is flung open by landlord.

LANDLORD:	'How many times do I have to say it – go away!'
JOSEPH:	'But ...'
LANDLORD:	'No buts – I've had people knocking on this door all night and I've got no room left. None at all.'
JOSEPH:	'But my wife, she's going to have a baby ...'
LANDLORD:	'That may be, but like I said – I've got no room at all.'
MARY *(faintly)*:	'Anywhere sir – anywhere at all would do. Just anywhere.'
LANDLORD:	'Look how many times ... wait a minute ...'
BEN:	'Oh no – here it comes!'
LANDLORD:	'Maybe I can help out after all – BEN!'
BEN:	'Yes, Dad.'
LANDLORD:	'Get down here quick.'

Ben appears in the doorway with Dad.

LANDLORD:	'I want you to take these two people to the stable round the corner. Clean it up a bit when you get there and make them comfortable.'
BEN:	'Yes, Dad.'
MARY:	'Thank you so much – both of you.'

End of Scene 1.

Scene 2: What was the outside of the inn has now become the inside of the stable. The door is open, a crib is in one corner with Mary and Joseph standing beside it. Ben is mid stage with a broom in his hand.

JOSEPH: 'Thank you lad, you've done a good job.'

BEN: 'Well at least it's clean, sir. The animals are out of the way (*Ben points off stage*) and you should have a quiet night.'

MARY: 'You've been very helpful, Ben.'

BEN: I'm going up to get more hay from the loft. Give me a shout if you want anything.'

Ben goes out of the door (and up to his window behind the stage); the curtains are drawn and behind the scenes everybody sings: 'Mary Had a Baby'. When the singing is over the curtains part. Mary and Joseph are kneeling by the crib where the new born baby now lies.)

BEN (*looking down from the window*):   'A new born baby – born in our stable. Hello – somebody is coming – I can hear them.'

A knock on the door – Joseph gets up and opens it.

SHEPHERD 1:   'You are here.'

JOSEPH (*puzzled*):   'Yes – who are you?'

SHEPHERD 2:   'We are the shepherds.'

SHEPHERD 3:   '...and we had a message to come here.'

JOSEPH: 'What sort of message?'

SHEPHERD 4:   'A fantastic message.'

SHEPHERD 1:   'The whole sky lit up over our flocks.'

SHEPHERD 2:   'Angels sang and told us that a king had been born ...'

SHEPHERD 3:   '...in a stable in Bethlehem.'

SHEPHERD 4:   'And so we have come with a gift.'

Boy shepherd comes in and presents lamb to Joseph and Mary. All shepherds kneel round crib in tableau scene. Off stage everyone sings 'Rise up Shepherds' or alternatively 'I Want to See Your Baby Boy.' Stable door remains open.

BEN (*when music stops and from window*): 'I've never seen anything like this – and somebody else is coming now. He's no older than me.'

A boy, the three kings' servant, enters through the door. Nobody notices him but Ben.

BEN: 'Psst – hey boy – come up here.'

KING'S SERVANT: 'Right – I'll be right with you.'

He goes out and the two boys appear together in the window.

KING'S SERVANT: 'I'm glad we're here. What a journey!'

BEN: 'Where have you come from?'

KING'S SERVANT: 'Far, far away.'

BEN:	'But why – and how did you find this little stable?'
KING'S SERVANT:	'I am a servant for three great kings. They got a message that a great king was to be born here tonight.'
BEN:	'But you still haven't told me how you got here.'

King's servant puts his arm round Ben's shoulders and points upwards.

KING'S SERVANT:	'Look – through that hole in the roof – what do you see?'
BEN:	'Why it's … it's a star – the brightest star I've ever seen!'
KING'S SERVANT:	'And …'
BEN:	'And it's right over this roof and as low as low can be!'
KING'S SERVANT:	'That's how we got here. We followed the star.'

Boy remains still and looking upwards while off stage 'Little Star' is sung.

BEN:	'Where are your kings then?'
KING'S SERVANT:	'They've brought wonderful presents for the new born baby. They'll be getting ready to bring them to him.'
BEN:	'Yes – they're coming now, I can see them.'

The three kings enter regally and in procession through the open door and kneel before the crib with their gifts. Mary stands and beckons the two boys to come down. They disappear, then come in through the door. Ben goes to Mary who puts her arm round him and leads him to look more closely at the baby in the crib. The whole scene is 'frozen' in tableau and everybody sings 'Mary Had a Baby' again to conclude the presentation.

2 Our Christmas

The point of this dramatic presentation is initially to focus on many of the things which make 'Our Christmas' – in the conventional modern sense – so enjoyable. The progression of the presentation leads however to an ending which focuses on the 'beginning' of it all.

Requirements for props and setting are basic. A simple Nativity scene should be hidden from view by a curtain or screens until the final denouement. Before this the characters involved can simply walk onto the stage (or presentation area) to say their piece and ultimately gather together. These characters can either be dressed in the role which they portray, or simply carry large pictures of those roles.

The presentation is arranged so that single characters alternate with groups in arriving on the scene. There is no difficulty in accommodating all the children in the class into this presentation.

Music
'Carol Singers' feature at one stage so it would be necessary for them to sing a carol.

The presentation could be introduced by everybody singing the very lively 'Christmas Time is Here.' This would be very appropriate to the forthcoming action.

The end – featuring the Nativity tableau – could be accompanied by either a taped version, or a live rendering of 'The Virgin Mary had a Baby Boy'.

Both of the latter carols are in *Come and Praise Vol 2*, BBC publications.

Characters

School party (four Party Goers)

Christmas Tree

Crackers (Three)

Father Christmas

Carol Singers (Four)

Parcel

Party Food (Four)

Christmas Card

Christmas Toys (Five)

Candle

Nativity Scene (Jesus, Mary and Joseph)

The characters (apart from those in the nativity scene) could be dressed in costume to show what they represent; or they could carry large pictures.

Action

'Christmas Time is Here' introduces the proceedings and when it is finished a group of Party Goers, children representing their class or school party appear.

PARTY GOER 1:   'School parties are great!'

PARTY GOER 2:   'I love the games we play.'

PARTY GOER 3:   'The food is yummy.'

PARTY GOER 4:   'Our teacher knows how to make a good party.'

PARTY GOER 1:   'One of the best things about Christmas is the school party.'

The group then retreat to a corner of the presenting area. The Christmas Tree comes on stage.

CHRISTMAS TREE: 'Hello, hello – where would you be without me? Everybody has a tree at Christmas. And don't I look good when the lights you hang on me are lit up? It wouldn't be Christmas without a tree!'

Christmas Tree joins Party Goers. Crackers come in next.

CRACKER 1:   'Pull!'

CRACKER 2:   'Bang!'

CRACKER 3:   'Plop!'

CRACKER 1:   'From me you might get a hat.'

CRACKER 2:   'Or from me a little toy.'

CRACKER 3:   'I'll give you a puzzle.'

ALL TOGETHER: 'Where would we be without crackers for Christmas?'

Crackers join Party Goers and Christmas Tree. Father Christmas enters.

FATHER CHRISTMAS: Ho, ho, ho. I'll be coming to your house soon – and yours – and yours.' (*He points indiscriminately at audience here.*) Everybody loves Father Christmas and why not – it's me who brings you all those lovely presents!'

Father Christmas joins static group. Carol Singers enter and sing a carol. They speak after the singing.

CAROL SINGER 1:   'At Christmas we hear the special sound of carols.'

CAROL SINGER 2:   'We hear them at school.'

CAROL SINGER 3:   '...at church...'

CAROL SINGER 4:   '...in the street...'

CAROL SINGER 1:   '...outside the supermarket....'

CAROL SINGER 2:   'The lovely sound of carols is everywhere at Christmas.'

Carol Singers join the group. Parcel enters.

PARCEL: 'I'm one of the great surprises at Christmas. I look beautiful in my special wrapping paper. But what's inside me? That's the exciting bit – opening me up and finding out.'

Parcel joins the group. Party Food group enters.

PARTY FOOD 1:   'I'm a mince pie – small and tasty.'

PARTY FOOD 2:   'I'm a jelly – bright and wobbly.'

PARTY FOOD 3:   'I'm a Christmas pudding – I'm very important.'

PARTY FOOD 4:   'I'm a Christmas log – covered in chocolate and beautifully decorated.'

ALL TOGETHER: Christmas party food is special!'

Party Food join the group. Christmas Card enters.

CHRISTMAS CARD: 'Aha – how many of me are there about at Christmas? I'll tell you – millions! How many of me are you going to send this year? Think how dull it would be without all those lovely Christmas cards.'

Card joins the group. Christmas Toys come in.

CHRISTMAS TOY 1:   'It wouldn't be Christmas without us toys, would it?'

CHRISTMAS TOY 2:   'There's dolls and footballs...'

CHRISTMAS TOY 3:   'Train sets and bikes...'

CHRISTMAS TOY 4:   'Computers and roller blades...'

CHRISTMAS TOY 5:   'Books and jigsaws...'

ALL TOGETHER: 'There's toys, toys, toys everywhere.'

Toys join group. Candle comes in.

CANDLE: 'You see lots of me at Christmas. But I want you to follow me. I'm going to show you why Christmas is really important. Look ... (*Candle goes, with candle held aloft, to the area where the Nativity had, up to now, been hidden. When Candle reaches it the scene is suddenly revealed. All now sing 'The Virgin Mary Had a Baby Boy.'*

3 A Star for Christmas

This is a mime to be enacted alongside a spoken commentary. Such a format can easily be adapted to incorporate a script if teachers decide this would be more effective. Once again props and stage settings are very basic. Costumes are predictable and can be effected without much difficulty – several 'stars', the Magi, the tableau setting of the Nativity group.

As 'a journey' needs to be made in this presentation a pathway round the hall, and possibly back up the middle, should be carefully laid out before proceedings begin.

Music
'We Three Kings of Orient Are' at a suitable processional pace is the key musical accompaniment here. 'O Little Town of Bethlehem' would be the most appropriate carol to sing at the end, when the 'journey to Bethlehem' has been completed.

Characters
Narrator (teacher/or adult or perhaps Year 6 pupil/s would be best here)

Group of Stars – one smaller and duller initially, but becoming 'brilliant'.

Messenger

The Magi

Nativity Scene Group (Jesus, Mary and Joseph)

Action
The presentation begins with a number of 'stars' milling around – one of their number is much smaller and duller than the rest.

NARRATOR: Long ago the stars gathered nightly in the dark sky. Some of them were big and bright and they didn't have much time for one particular star. He was much smaller than the rest and didn't shine half as brightly.

The other stars were rude to him and made jokes about how dull he was. Then, one night, a special messenger came to see the stars.

Enter Messenger. Actions match the narrative which follows.

NARRATOR: 'Good evening, stars,' said the Messenger. 'I have come with some very important news. One of you is to be chosen to make a very special journey. He has to lead three great kings to a small town where the greatest king of all is going to be born.'

The big, bright stars tried to push each other out of the way. They all wanted to be chosen by the Messenger to be the special star.

'This is a job for me,' sparkled the brightest star.

'I can move faster than any of you,' boasted a very sharp pointed star.

'Only the biggest star can do this job,' boomed the very biggest star.

Right away at the back, pushed almost out of sight, was the poor dull little star.

'Oh dear,' he sighed. 'I don't suppose the messenger will even notice me.'

Then he got an enormous surprise.

The Messenger moved through all the other stars. Pushing them gently out of the way he reached the small, dull star.

'You, my friend,' he said. 'You are the one who must do this important job.'

The little star couldn't believe his ears.

'Thank you – oh thank you,' he whispered. Then he went even duller than usual, 'But I'm so small and dull the kings will never even see me in the sky.'

'He's quite right there,' sneered the biggest star.

'Aha,' said the Messenger. 'That's something we're going to put right now. Come with me.'

At this point Messenger and little, dull star leave the stage, returning almost immediately with the 'little' star now brighter and bigger than all the others.

'Now,' said the Messenger. 'Your great journey must begin. You must lead the three kings to Bethlehem.'

Stars leave the presenting area. The three kings take their place – to the first introductory music of 'We Three Kings'.

NARRATOR: The kings made ready for their journey to Bethlehem. But they were puzzled. How were they going to find their way? A star was supposed to guide them – but which star?

They gazed at the sky, and then suddenly they saw one star which was bigger and brighter than all the others. It was also moving and seemed to be saying: 'Follow me.'

At this point the star 'appears' again and begins to move round the hall. The three kings follow with all the verses of 'We Three Kings' being sung. Finally the procession reaches the pre-arranged part of the hall where curtains/screens are removed to reveal a Nativity tableau.

NARRATOR: And so the star led the three kings on their great journey to Bethlehem. There in a tiny stable they found the great king they had come to worship. Bringing their wonderful gifts they gave thanks for the birth of the baby Jesus.

So, with all involved now in the tableau setting the proceedings end with the singing of 'O Little Town of Bethlehem'.

8 'All the Things We Are' – Christmas and other cultures

(Activity sheets 26 and 27)

Young children in multi-cultural classes, and those which embrace work on different cultures, gain an enormous amount by their experience. If we consider 'multi-cultural' at this level to be a judicious mixture of story, celebration, visual and aural impact, with side issues of drama, food, costume etc., thrown in, then it is hardly surprising that much enjoyment is engendered!

Luckily Christmas with other cultures can be done in various ways. There are several themes which allow positive links to be made. Obvious ones are 'Light and Darkness' whereby the Jewish Festival of Light (Hanukkah) and the Hindu Festival of Diwali could be included. 'Beginnings' could link Christmas with the Buddhist celebration of Bodhi Day when Prince Gautama discovered enlightenment under the Bodhi tree, and the Muslim Day of Hijrah when a 'beginning' was made with Mohammad's flight from Mecca to Medina. 'Birthdays' is another very appropriate theme and could involve the birth of Guru Nanak, founder of the Sikh religion; the Hindu festival of Janam Ashtami which celebrates the birth of Lord Krishna; and Meelad-ul-Nabi, the Muslim festival celebrating the birth of Mohammad.

A less obvious 'theme' but an informative and enjoyable one would be 'Food'. Here the Christmas fare of pudding, mince pies, jelly and cake could be linked with the potato pancakes (latkes) of Hanukkah; the curries which Buddhist layfolk present to their monks at the Wesak festival when the birth, enlightenment and death of the Buddha are celebrated; and the chocolate, sweets and cakes of Diwali.

Other links could have story examples from the various cultures, examples of different greetings cards, a comparison and contrasting of pictures and symbols, samples of different songs and musical offerings.

At a practical level a 'multi-cultural' corner linked to the Christmas features in the Infant classroom could be an intriguing resource area.

This chapter therefore seeks to provide practical help in achieving any of the features already mentioned. In order to do this the following approach has been taken. Under the heading of each other culture there is:

a some basic background information for the teacher.

b some suggestions which might help with an 'exhibition corner' – recipes, food, visual ideas, music.

c one story which can be read to the children as an example of tales from that particular culture.

The chapter ends with a suggested assembly involving a multi-cultural theme.

There are two activity sheets (nos 26 and 27) related to the work contained in this chapter.

Hinduism

Background information

The two most obvious Hindu festivals for linking with Christmas are Diwali and Janam Ashtami.

The main feature of Diwali is the story of Rama and Sita. The *Ramayana* is the epic poem which tells this story. In it Prince Rama wins the hand of Princess Sita by stringing a giant bow which requires one hundred and fifty men to carry it. After the wedding, however, Bharata, Rama's brother, is proclaimed King after his mother, one of the three wives of King Dasharatha, reminds the King that this is what he has promised her.

Rama, Sita and Lakshmana (Rama's other brother) put on poor clothes and go to live in a hut in the forest. They are happy until the evil Ravana kidnaps Sita. With the help of the monkey god Hanuman, Rama eventually rescues his wife and, after fourteen years, returns to the throne of Ayodhya. Great celebrations mark this triumph of 'Light over Darkness'.

Janam Ashtami celebrates the birth of Lord Krishna. This came about when Vishnu, the Creator of everything, plucked a black hair from his head – and created Krishna from it.

Exhibition suggestions

Food

Food is an important feature of the Diwali celebrations. Basically it falls into two categories – 'hot and spicy' or 'sweet and thick'. The latter feature milk as a basic ingredient because in legend the goddess Lakshmi was created from a sea of milk.

It would be a very exciting feature of a 'multi-cultural' corner if some Burfi chocolate could be on display – even more so if there was enough to be eaten. Where applicable many parents will be able to help here. A recipe for this chocolate is as follows:

Requirements

8oz khoa (dried fresh whole milk)

$\frac{1}{2}$ oz cocoa

silver leaves (optional)

$2\frac{1}{2}$ oz castor sugar

$\frac{1}{2}$ oz butter (use only if khoa is dry)

Technique

1 Divide the khoa into two parts. Heat one part over slow fire. Mash and add 1oz fine sugar. Stir well and heat until it dries up. Remove from the fire, cool slightly and spread over a greased thali (tray) or greaseproof paper.

2 Heat the remaining half of the khoa over slow fire, mash and add cocoa powder and $1\frac{1}{2}$ oz of sugar. Add $\frac{1}{2}$ oz butter if the khoa is not sufficiently greasy. Stir till all the ingredients are thoroughly mixed.

3 Remove the mixture from the fire, cool a little, and spread it over the khoa-sugar on the tray.

4 Decorate with silver leaf (optional) and leave it to set.

5 Cut into diamond pieces after it becomes firm. Keep in an airtight tin.

The food link can also be carried over to Janam Ashtami celebrations because traditionally special sweets were put in Lord Krishna's cradle on this occasion.

Visual material

It is relatively easy these days to obtain some Diwali greetings cards. These could be contrasted with Christmas cards. They usually feature divas (the lamps lit to celebrate Rama's triumphant return) on the front with the traditional 'Happy Diwali and best wishes for the New Year' inside. A draped Sari would also be an attractive feature.

It might also be useful to show the great sacred symbol of Hinduism. All Hindu prayers begin with the syllable Om, shown as:

Finally in this visual section it would be fun to look at the symbols which represent the game of Ikki Dukki. This is the Indian version of hopscotch and the symbols in the squares represent universes, oceans and heavens, e.g.

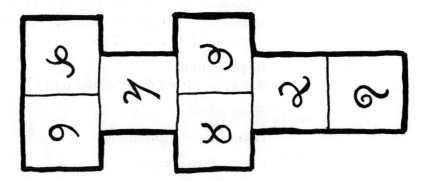

Singing

The children would enjoy a tape of 'Hari Krishna' being sung. Even more so they would enjoy singing it themselves – with the addition of some tinkling little bells, and the ever increasing tempo. The following simple melody might help with the latter:

The leader sings the theme first. The congregation follow. The song is repeated. The more times it is repeated, the faster it gets.

Dance

Hindu hand movements in dance focus are very expressive – and also easy and enjoyable for young children to perform.

For instance, to use the hands to indicate birds in flight, the right wrist is crossed over the left with the palms facing upwards. Thumbs are then linked and the hands moved up and down to portray a bird in flight.

To symbolise a fish swimming, the right hand is placed on top of the left – with both hands facing downwards. The two thumbs are then 'wriggled' to indicate fin movement of the fish.

In connection with this material it is well worth looking in the school's musical books section to see if *Every Colour Under the Sun* (songs on thoughtful themes for primary school assemblies, published by Ward Lock Educational), is there. This is a marvellously varied book with much very suitable Key Stage 1 material.

It contains a song entitled 'Kishnay Baniya Ion Ko?' (phonetically written here and meaning – 'Who made the flowers red and white?') This is very easy to sing and play and incorporates detailed instructions for accompanying hand and arm dance movements such as those described here.

A Hindu story

(*Teacher's note*: The story here is a re-telling of part of the Ramayana. It would be advantageous if the teacher could 'set the scene'. Ravana has kidnapped Sita from the hut in the forest and taken her to his island kingdom of Lanka. Rama and Lakshmana are in pursuit, with Hanuman, Leader (God) of the monkeys helping them …)

Journey with the monkeys

'This is a terrible journey,' said Rama.

'Well, we've certainly come a long way,' replied his brother. 'Over mountains, through forests. Past towns.'

'Yes, and we've still got a long way to go,' added Hanuman.

All around Rama and Lakshmana were hundred and thousands of monkeys. They didn't just walk either! Some of them ran ahead doing handsprings and cartwheels, others played leapfrog with each other as they went along. They climbed trees and shouted and laughed. There were so many of them that a great cloud of dust seemed to surround them.

Finally they reached the sea shore. Out of sight and far away over the sea lay Lanka. Here Ravana had the captured Sita.

Rama and Lakshmana stood on the shore. It was night and the moon shone down on the waves. Gazing along the moonlit path along the water Rama spoke to his brother.

'How are we ever going to get across this sea?' he said sadly.

'I don't know,' muttered Lakshmana. 'It seems impossible to me.'

'Don't say that, my friends,' said Hanuman, who had come up behind the two brothers. 'I have spoken to Nala, who builds great bridges. He will help us.'

And so the next morning Nala spoke to all the thousands and thousands of monkeys.

'My friends,' he said. 'We must build a great bridge over the sea. To do this we must have trees and rocks and stones. Let's get busy.'

So the monkeys swarmed over the shore and the mountainside. They pulled up great trees by the roots. They rolled huge rocks down the mountainside and into the sea. They piled millions of stones one of top of another. Soon a great bridge began to stretch out into the sea ahead. They were on their way to Lanka.

(N.B. Nala was the son of the architect of the Gods who had in fact built Lanka itself.

The teacher could conclude the story simply (although in fact it has many complexities in the original) by saying that eventually the bridge was built and, after a battle, Sita was rescued.)

Judaism Background information

Hanukkah is the Jewish Festival of Light. Like Diwali it occurs just before the Christian Christmas so its timing as well as its theme is most appropriate for 'linking' purposes.

Hanukkah celebrates the miraculous happenings of over two thousand years ago. At that time Judas Maccabee led a resurgence of the Jews against their oppressors, the Syrians. After their victory the Jews repaired their Temple but found only a very small quantity of oil with which to light the Temple lamp. Miraculously their oil kept the lamp burning for eight days – the period which Hanukkah lasts, in remembrance of this great event.

Exhibition suggestions

Food

Potato pancakes – latkes or blintzes (traditionally made with cheese) – are especially eaten at Hanukkah. Again, with parental help these could be made, but a more permanent, and much more beguiling use of food here would be to provide an example of the popular Jewish game which uses a dreidel as its main feature. This is played during the festivities of Hanukkah in the following way.

Each player starts with 15 sweets or nuts or raisins. At the start of each game he/she puts one of these into the middle – 'the pot'. One player then spins the dreidel. This is a spinning top with four sides. Each side has a Jewish letter on it.

If it lands with the letter uppermost, the player has to add two more sweets to the pot.

If the letter is uppermost then the player gets half the pot.

If appears the whole pot is won.

If appears then the player gets nothing.

The game then moves on to the next player and so on.

Obviously all young children enjoy playing this game and spinning the top is good for increasing dexterity. From the teacher's point of view it might be of interest to know that during the many periods of persecution of the Jews a game of dreidel was often used as a 'cover'. This group of Jews – suspiciously huddled together and apparently in deep conversation – could be 'revealed' as doing nothing more sinister than playing a harmless game of dreidel.

Visual material

In view of the links with Christmas then some representation of a Jewish candle holder would be most appropriate here. With young children it is sufficient to light a candle for each of the eight days of celebration – perhaps again linking with Christmas the idea of light, good, remembering a very special time, etc.

The menorah is the traditional seven branched candle holder found in Jewish synagogues. The eight-branched candle holder used for celebrating Hanukkah is called the Hanukkiah. Traditionally the candles are lit immediately after sunset and must burn for an hour. As the candles are lit Jews remember that the light from them must serve no other purpose then to remind them of the miracle being celebrated.

Music

The BBC *Come and Praise Vol. 2* is a feast of riches. This book which is very popular in schools and is readily available, contains a simple traditional version of 'Shalom' which can be sung as a round.

Geoffrey Gardner has also used another traditional tune and fitted 'festival words' round it. These are 'Christmas Time is Here' or 'Hanukkah is Here' (or indeed 'Diwali is Here'). Once again the melody is very simple to play and, whichever version of the words is used, young children enjoy the whole thing enormously.

Finally 'Flickering Candles in the Night' is designated as being for use at either Hanukkah, Christmas or Diwali. This is another piece which is very easy to play on the piano and the words are delightful to use with Key Stage 1 children.

A Jewish story

How Rich Are You?

Jacob and Michael were two boys who were born in the same village. They were friends at school. As they grew up they talked about all sorts of things. One day Jacob asked Michael a question.

'What are you going to do when you grow up?' he said.

Michael thought for a moment.

'Well – I'd like to get a job in the village, and one day have a home of my own.'

Jacob gave a great laugh.

'Is that all?' he said. 'You know what I'm going to do when I grow up – I'm going to be rich – that's what I'm going to be.'

So the two boys grew up. Michael got a job in a shop in the village. He knew all the customers. They all knew him. He was always polite and helpful and everybody liked him. He saved some of his wages and after he had got married, he bought a little house in the village. He was very happy.

Then one day he got some news.

'Have you heard?' asked a lady in the shop. 'Jacob's coming to the village this weekend. You remember Jacob – he's always on TV now. Rich and famous, he is.'

'Oh yes, I remember Jacob,' answered Michael. 'He and I were great friends.'

That night Michael got a telephone call from his old friend Jacob.

'I'd love to have a meal with you when I come to the village,' said Jacob.

'That will be marvellous,' replied Michael. 'It'll be just like old times.'

So Jacob arrived. He was wearing beautiful clothes and he had a big, expensive car.

Michael and his wife Sarah made him very welcome, and they all had a lovely meal.

'Well my old friend, why don't you stay the night with us?' asked Michael.

'I'd like to,' replied Jacob. 'But I've got to get back to the city tonight. I've got an important business meeting which is going to make me a lot of money.'

Jacob paused, and then he smiled. 'Remember what I used to say when we were young – I was going to get rich when I grew up.'

Now it was Michael's turn to smile. 'I remember, but I think I'm richer than you are, my old friend.'

Jacob looked surprised. 'But – how can you say that?'

'Well,' answered Michael. 'I've got all the money I want – but you obviously haven't.'

(An adaptation of a Jewish story)

Buddhism

Background information

A Buddhist link with Christmas could be twofold, via 'Brides' or 'Gifts'. The Buddhist festival of Wesak celebrates the birth, enlightenment and death of the Buddha. Perhaps his 'enlightenment' is the most significant here. It came as he sat and meditated under a tree, which became known as the 'bodhi' ('wisdom') tree. After a life of indulgence the Buddha now understood the meaning of existence.

Buddhist monks keep the Dharma (teachings of the Buddha) alive. At Wesak they receive gifts from the people. These are specially prepared curries. In return the monks give gifts to the people in the form of 'advice' from the Buddha's teachings. A further 'gift' in the overall participation in this ceremony is that of a 'good deed' by those who help feed the monks. This in turn will help the giver to have a better rebirth on his next entry into life.

Exhibition suggestions

Food

Young children are not always enthusiastic curry eaters so perhaps a delicately prepared bowl of rice might be the food to try here. Other things particularly associated with Buddhist festivals are iced coconut milk, rice cakes and sweet bean paste pancakes. Parental help, if available, would of course be valuable here.

Visual suggestions

The 'light' theme is again a strong link and at the Wesak festival many lights are placed round statues of the Buddha. The Buddha also taught that Buddhism is like a boat which carries its believers over the sea of ignorance. In consequence Buddhists have a 'floating candle' festival in which boats made from leaves are decorated with a burning joss-stick and then floated on rivers.

This could be reproduced in the display section by making a simple boat or raft from some leaves. This could be put in a bowl of water and a small candle or joss stick fixed in it. The latter could be lit as and when the teacher wanted to draw attention to it.

Another useful artefact would be an empty bird cage – to remind viewers that at Wesak caged birds were set free in memory of the Buddha's kindness.

Elephants feature largely in Buddhist celebrations (and in Buddhist stories) so the final display feature could be a model, or picture, of an elephant.

Music and dance

As with the comments on hand movements in Hindu dance, Buddhist festivals in Thailand in particular are often characterised by stylised dance. Movement and gestures of hands have important meanings and finger caps with long nails attached emphasise these.

Shadow plays are also popular. A very simple example using a sheet, a light and a cut out figure could be shown to the children here. These are usually accompanied by loud noises from gongs and cymbals – there should be no shortage of volunteers wishing to participate!

A Buddhist story

The Bandit

Long, long ago the people who lived in a town in India were very frightened. This town was called Savatthi. One day a very wise man came to visit the town. He was called the Buddha.

'Oh dear,' said one of the townspeople to the Buddha. 'I wish you had come at a happier time.'

'Oh,' replied the Buddha. 'Why is that?'

'You mean you haven't heard about the bandit?'

'No,' said the Buddha, stroking his chin. 'Perhaps you'd better tell me all about him.'

So a great crowd of people gathered round the wise man. One after the other they told him about the bandit.

'The bandit lives outside the city.'

'He is the worst robber we've ever known.'

'Whenever anybody leaves the city, he hides and waits for them.'

'Yes … and then he robs them.'

'We're all terrified of this bandit.'

Once again the Buddha stroked his chin. Then he smiled.

'Well I'll have to do something about this bandit, won't I?'

The next morning when the sun was up the Buddha went to the edge of the city. A great crowd of people went with him. They called out.

'Take care Lord, the bandit is dangerous.'

'Don't you want somebody to come with you?'

The Buddha waved a quiet farewell. Then he was outside the city and walking over the hot, dusty country road.

From his hideout high above the city the bandit had watched everything that had happened.

'This man's a fool,' he thought to himself, 'but I daresay he'll have something worth stealing.'

So the bandit buckled on his huge sword. Then he hid in the place where he waited for all his victims. He heard the Buddha's dragging footsteps getting closer and closer. Then …

'Stop!' cried the bandit, as he leapt out into the road. 'I'll have your money now!'

To the bandits astonishment the Buddha didn't appear to hear him – or even notice him in fact. He just kept walking on at the same pace.

'Stop… didn't you hear what I said?' snarled the bandit.

But he was talking to thin air. The Buddha had already walked past him.

'I'll teach him a lesson!' thought the bandit. Then with a great roar he leapt after the Buddha. But an amazing thing happened.

As the bandit rushed after him, the Buddha just seemed to get further and further away. Soon the bandit was running flat out – and although the Buddha still just appeared to be strolling away, he couldn't catch him.

Over the long, hot, dusty trail the bandit chased the Buddha. All the while he was shouting terrible things, but then, suddenly, he had no breath left. Dropping his sword, he sank to the ground. Then to his surprise he saw that the Buddha had stopped too – and was walking back towards him.

'Well,' said the Buddha. 'I've stopped – now, will you?'

'What do you mean?' blustered the bandit.

'Will you stop being a bandit and robbing people?'

For a few minutes the bandit looked at the Buddha – then he suddenly thought what an awful person he had been.

'You're… you're right,' he said. 'I've robbed people, and hurt them. But how can I put it right?'

As he said this the bandit fell on his knees in front of the Buddha.

'What you must do is this,' answered the Buddha. 'Take back to the people in the town all the things you have stolen from them. Tell them how sorry you are. Then ask if you can live in the town, and try to do everything you can to show you are now a kind and thoughtful man.'

So the bandit went back to Savatthi. At first the people were frightened when they saw him. Then they realised how sorry he was about being a robber – and so he lived with them for the rest of his life as a friend and a good neighbour.

Islam · Background information

Using 'birth' as the link between Christmas and Muslim celebrations, then Meelad-ul-Nabi, the birthday of the Prophet Muhammad, born in AD 570, can be featured in this section. Not only is Muhammad's birthday celebrated by Muslims, but the whole month of his birth is considered very significant. Ceremonial readings from the Qur'an take place, along with prayers and stories of his life.

When a baby is born into a Muslim family the father whispers the Adhan (the call to prayer) in his right ear. This welcomes the child into the faith.

Another link with Christmas could be via 'journeys' and the connection here could be the journey to Mecca (Al Hajj) which all Muslims try to make once in their lifetime.

Exhibition suggestions

Food

Food is obviously most significant at Eid-ul-Fitr, the festival celebrating the end of Ramadan, the month of fasting. All meals are special at Eid-ul-Fitr but the one young children probably like best is tea time. This is no doubt heightened by the fact that this is usually present-opening time too!

Coconut cakes, almond-stuffed dates and sweets of aniseed flavoured icing sugar are likely to be on the menu. Once again parental help in producing some examples would be invaluable here.

Visual material

An attractive display of a few Eid-ul-Fitr cards could be displayed to show examples of another culture's greetings cards. Some plain white material might also be on display, as a reminder of what all Muslims must wear when they make their pilgrimage to Mecca.

In classes where there are few or no Muslim children, then some cards showing common names could be informative. These might include Abd Allah (which means 'servant of God'), Muhammad, Ali and Husein. These are all boys' names and the last two are after members of Muhammad's family. A selection of girls' names might include Sharifa which means 'noble', or some more which reflect the Prophet's family – Aisha, Khadija and Fatima.

For those schools which have links with Muslim families it might be possible to borrow a prayer mat for the children to look at. A photograph or model of a mosque would also be a useful display item.

Sounds

Once again the BBC's *Come and Praise Vol. 2* is useful here because Geoffrey Gardner's 'multi-cultural' hymn (no. 27) can be sung with the words – 'The Prophet's Day is Here.'

Other sounds which are 'different' might include a Muslim call to prayer. Local contacts might again be useful here and some time ago Argo records produced 'Religions of the Middle East' which included a muezzin's call.

In Islamic countries the firing of a canon announces the beginning and end of Ramadan, so there are possibilities for some interesting 'sound effects' work with the children in this context!

An Islamic story

A Tall story

The Hodja had lent his very big cooking pan to a friend.

'I have got a big party this week,' said the friend, 'and I've got a lot of cooking to do. Your big pan would be very helpful.'

'Certainly,' said the Hodja. 'I'll be happy to lend it to you.'

So the Hodja loaned his pan out. After four weeks he had still not got it back. Two more weeks went by, and then two more. The pan still had not come back. The Hodja went to see his friend.

'Ali,' he said. 'You said you wanted to borrow my pan for a week – and you've had it eight weeks. I've been needing it desperately. Can I have it back please?'

'Oh. … oh,' replied Ali, rubbing his hand over his face, and looking very guilty. 'Oh … there was a very good reason I haven't given it back to you.'

'What's that?' asked the Hodja.

'Well – look!'

As he spoke, the friend got the Hodja's pan down from a shelf. Inside it was another pan – a very very small one.

'You see,' went on Ali, 'while I had your pan – it had a baby.'

'Had a …' began the startled Hodja. Then he took his pan and went off without another word.

Well, it so happened that six months later Ali called on the Hodja again.

'My friend,' he said. 'I've got another big party coming up – can I borrow your lovely big cooking pan again please.'

The Hodja looked at his friend, and then he let out a long sad, sigh.'

'I'm so sorry Ali,' he said, 'but the pan has died.'

(N.B. A little guidance from the teacher might be necessary for the children to get the point of this story. It is included here however because the 'Hodja stories' are a marvellous source of entertainment and subtle moral guidance.)

Nasr-ud-Din was a great legendary hero of the Middle East. Quick thinking and witty, he may have lived in the 14th or 15th century. Such was his fame that he was given the honorary title of Hodja. This term means someone with great knowledge of the Qur'an. A Hodja may be a Khatib – a preacher in a mosque, an Imam (prayer leader) or a Cadi (magistrate).

Sikhism

Background information

Guru Nanak's birthday is a possible link with Christmas via a 'birth' theme. The 'light' and 'dark' aspects feature largely too because the word 'guru' is very significant. It has come to mean 'teacher' but the two syllables 'gu' and 'ru' stand for 'dark' and 'light' respectively. Thus when a man is a 'guru' he leads his subjects from darkness to light by increasing their understanding.

Guru Nanak, the founder of Sikhism, was born in the Punjab in 1469. Confused as to whether he should be a Hindu or a Muslim, Nanak realised after meditation that he must simply follow God – who was neither Hindu nor Muslim. Others followed his ideas and teachings, and became the first Sikhs.

Exhibition suggestions

Food

It would be useful if a small selection of flour, butter, sugar and water could be on show for the children to see. The significance of these are as follows, (and in some cases the teacher may wish to continue to the cooking of the ingredients).

For 48 hours prior to Guru Nanak's birthday, Sikhs gather in their gurdwara to worship by reading the holy book – Guru Granth Sahib. Meanwhile in the kitchen of the gurdwara the ingredients above are heated together and mixed with a sword (kirpan). A large bowl of the mixture is then taken round and everyone samples it with their fingers.

Visual material

As Sikhs are most readily recognisable by their turbans it would be useful to have a photograph and/or turban on display.

Alongside these could be a kanga, the comb which Sikhs use to keep their uncut hair tidy, and a sword-shaped brooch. The children would enjoy the significance of the latter. The five symbols of Sikhism are the five Ks – one of which is the kirpan – a sword which they should wear at all times. As this would be very difficult in modern Britain they wear instead the sword-shaped brooch – often pinned to their turban.

Music

Hospitality is very important to Sikhs and nowhere is this more evident than in the sharing of food at the celebration of Guru Nanak's birthday.

It might therefore be appropriate for the children to listen to Sydney Carter's well known hymn 'I Come Like a Beggar'. Although not specifically to do with Sikhism its theme is one of sharing and caring which is very much in keeping with this particular festival. It can be played easily by an average pianist. One source is *Come and Praise Vol. 2*.

An alternative choice, and in keeping with Guru Nanak's belief that 'God was simply God' might be to sing the well known 'He's Got the Whole World in His Hands'.

A Sikh story

The Present

Guru Nanak lived a very long time ago. He was such a kind man that other people often gave him presents. Now, when the Guru got these presents he always said the same thing to himself.

'I've got so much, and people are so kind. I wonder if I can use what they have given me to help somebody else?'

One day the Guru went to stay in a village. He talked to all the villagers and he sat outside under a shady tree so that anybody could come to see him.

In the village was a man who was very clever at making carpets. He had nearly finished making one of his very best ones.

'I've got a wonderful idea,' he thought. 'When I've finished this carpet I'll give it to Guru Nanak. Then he will always have something comfortable to sit on.'

So the carpet maker sat late into the night and finished his magnificent carpet. The next morning he carried it through the village to where Guru Nanak was already sitting in the pale morning sun.

'Sir,' said the carpet maker, 'would you please take this present from me? Then you will always have somewhere comfortable to sit.'

Guru Nanak looked at the carpet maker and smiled.

'My friend,' he replied, 'you are so very, very kind and I can't thank you enough for your beautiful present. But I am quite comfortable sitting on the grass and I think your magnificent carpet is desperately needed over there.'

When he said this the Guru pointed to his right. A little distance away lay a poor dog which had just given birth to some tiny puppies. It was shivering and terribly thirsty.

'You are right, Sir,' said the carpet maker. So he took his carpet and laid it over the dog and its puppies and then he went off to get them some food and milk.

Guru nodded his head and smiled. Kindness is a wonderful thing.

(Activity sheet 27 refers specifically to this story.)

'All the things we are': A multi-cultural assembly

In seeking to emphasise the varied aspects of its theme this assembly could be produced by having the class split up into groups and in different places in the hall. This arrangement might look as follows:

The assembly could then begin by everybody singing a very well known Christmas carol. At the end of this, Group 1 speaks in chorus:

'Christmas is a wonderful time. We celebrate Jesus being born. We have fun! Here are some things to remind you of Christmas.'

At this stage the children in the group hold up a number of artefacts familiar to Christmas. These might include such things as cards, crackers, decorations, crib figures, parcels, holly etc.

As soon as this has been done Group 2 makes their announcement. 'Diwali is a wonderful time. We celebrate the story of Rama and Sita. We have fun! Here are some things to remind you of Diwali.'

Once again the children flourish a selection of things which could have been collected for the display area as described in the previous part of this section.

So the assembly could proceed. Each group could use the same choral words – with the name of the festival being adjusted on each occasion. A selection of things could then be shown to reflect each culture. 'Sounds' could replace or add to visual aspects.

Then Group 3 could reflect on Judaism, Group 4 Buddhism, Group 5 Sikhism, and Group 6 Islam.

When each of these little cameos is complete the teacher could say something. Obviously this will depend on the composition and variable knowledge of the school and the area it is in, but the teacher's words could draw together the feelings of celebration, of sharing festivals, of symbols by which we recognise them, of the joy of participation.

The detail of this assembly has been left deliberately 'loose' because for a celebration of this nature so much depends of the environment of the school. Those with strong multi-cultural affiliations will obviously have many more resources to draw on, but classes and schools without these advantages could still find this approach a stimulating addition to their Christmas 'progress'.

For those teachers who are particularly interested in the suggestions of this chapter, the following addresses and references may be useful:

Hinduism
Hindu Centre, 7 Cedars Road, London E15 4NE.

ISCON Educational Services, Bhakti Vedanta Manor, Letchworth, Herts. WD2 8ED.

Judaism
Jewish Education Bureau, 8 Westcombe Avenue, Leeds L58 2BS.

Council of Christians and Jews, 48 Onslow Gardens, London SW7 3PX.

Islam
Iqra Trust, 24 Culross Street, London W1Y 3HE.

Muslim Educational Trust, 130 Stroud Green Road, London N4 3RZ.

Buddhism
The Jataka tales are a valuable source of Buddhist stories.

Buddhist Society, 58 Eccleston Square, London SW1V 1PH.

Sikhism
The Sikh Cultural Society, 17 Abbotshill Road, Catford, London SE6 1SQ.

The Sikh Missionary Society, 20 Peacock Street, Gravesend, Kent.

The RE Centre, National Society (Church of England) for Promoting Religious Education, 23 Kensington Square, London W8 5HN distributes the invaluable annual journal of the SHAP Working Party on World Religions in Education.

The Independent Publishing Company, 38 Kennington Lane, London SE11 4LS publish a large number of cards, posters and books of multi-cultural interest.

Music

Music now pervades Christmas in such a way as to demean its overall appeal – as for instance the synthesised commercial outpourings which greet us in supermarkets from early December onwards.

Despite this, Key Stage 1 children derive great pleasure from music which they associate with Christmas in school. This can basically be divided into three categories: carols, music for plays and shows, and music to listen to.

Carols

St Francis of Assissi is credited as the first man to link specific songs to the events of the first Christmas. When he established his crib in Italy in the thirteenth century he also wrote songs which, when sung, would complement what he was presenting in a visual way.

Of the many carols which have been written since then a surprising number of those popular in infant schools come from the United States of America. 'O Little Town of Bethlehem', 'Away in a manger' and 'We Three Kings' are examples, all stemming from the mid 1800s.

New, and very good, carols are appearing all the time so apart from the traditional 'bank' like those above which all schools have, there is a steady flow from new anthologies. Rather than offer suggestions of carols, therefore, (apart from those already recommended throughout the book where linked to various assemblies, activities, etc.,) some thought on how to use the repertoire to the greatest advantage might be most useful.

With so many multi-cultural classes in modern infant schools there is much to be said for using carols in thematic collections. These could be grouped round such universal themes as Homes, Families, Journeys, Giving, Celebrating, Light and Sharing.

Similarly when gathering for assemblies during December there is a great deal of pleasure in each class offering a rendering of 'their carol' as well as the community singing of a favourite. This increases the children's overall awareness of carols and adds to the feeling of sharing something special.

Many easy carols lend themselves to clapped or percussion accompaniments and these should not be neglected. There is also a need for young children to hear carols beautifully sung – by other children or adults – and suggestions of these follow in 'Music to listen to'.

Music for plays and shows

Key Stage 1 teachers are always searching for that elusive material to perform with their children – easy but entrancing music, visual appeal, suitable words, a satisfying spectacle.

In this context contact should be made initially with the Music Sales Group, Education Department, Newmarket Road, Bury St. Edmonds, Suffolk IP33 3YB. (Telephone: 01284 702600, fax: 01284 768301). This group markets music and shows from publishers such as Chester Music, Golden Apple Productions, Novello, Shawnee Press, Youngsong Musicals and Wide World Music.

Between them they have, for years, been producing top class material, much of it specially aimed at the Key Stage 1 age range. To give examples of the riches available from this source details of some of their material are as follows:

Baby Jesus
Lasting for 25 minutes, this traditional story (written by Alison Hedger) contains seven carols ('A Girl Called Mary, Shepherds were Looking After Baby Lambs, A Special Star' among them), easy piano and percussion parts, a teacher's book and cassette. It is suitable for children up to 7.

Little Lost Kitten
By Caroline Hoile and edited by Alison Hedger, this piece is also suitable for children up to 7. Once again there is a teacher's book and cassette; suggestions for mime, movement and dance and original songs such as 'Miaow, Miaow,' and 'Oh Where You?' The action takes place on Christmas Eve.

Other publications with the same sort of festive, moral but original approach and suitability for up to 7 years old are: *Little Angel, Happy Christmas Everyone, Grumpy Sheep, Gold, Frankincense and Myrrh,* and *Gigantic Star.*

The Music Sales Group also produce excellent carol anthologies – some of which are many years old, others new. Of the former *Fifteen European Carols* by A W Benoy contains some beautiful music. *Sing Song,* 25 new Christmas songs, has the advantage of being written by teachers for their pupils. While things such as 'Christmas Bells', 'Mary had a Message', and 'One Bright Star' are traditionally linked there is also secular material here. Alison Hedges is the guiding hand behind this anothology.

Others to consider might be *A Feast of Easy Carols No. 1* by Carol Barratt, and *Carols to Sing, Clap and Play* by Heather Cox and Garth Rickard.

It is unlikely that a query to Musical Sales Group will meet with disappointment!

Music to listen to

The 'live' option is the first one to consider here. Infants love watching and listening to their counterparts performing in the Junior School so no opportunities should be missed here. Similarly, an approach to a nearby secondary school is usually sympathetically received. If this can result in a visit from a secondary choir (and instrumental accompanists) giving a short and appropriate performance then this would be a great asset.

From the recorded music point of view, currently available material and suitable playing equipment are two major considerations. Cassettes are valuable in that they can be used for whole school listening or taken to the classroom for the benefit of a lesser audience.

Some good cassettes from the Music Sales Group (see above) are:

Everywhere, Everywhere, Christmas Tonight by Steve Kupferschmid. This is a trip round the world via Christmas music and customs. Ten different countries are visited. Cassette reference: SP 16264.

Two other possibilities from the same source are very different. The first reflects the Christmas season without reference to religious aspects; the second is Tiny Tim's musical viewpoint of Dickens' *A Christmas Carol.* These two cassettes are:

Teddy Bean, Snowflakes, Candles and Bells by Joyce Merman, Cassette SP 19797.

Tiny Tim's Christmas Carol by James Leisy and Joyce Merman, Cassette SP 19847.

It would be valuable to buy or borrow a version of Menotti's *Amahl and the Night Visitors.* Very short passages would of course be best for Key Stage 1 listening but it is the juxtaposition of music and story which is so intriguing in the opera. Written originally for American children's television, this is the story of Amahl, a crippled boy who is the son of a shepherdess. He is visited by the Magi and invites them in for a rest. When he hears of their mission he too wants to present a gift to the Christ Child and all he can offer is his crutch. As a result of his action his lameness is cured and he joins the Kings on their journey.

If funds run to buying a new CD for Christmas listening, then there is much to recommend getting one of the choir of the King's College Chapel, Cambridge. These are usually readily available and it is worth watching papers like the *Daily Telegraph* for special offers. The quality is guaranteed and young children enjoy hearing about their slightly older counterparts who have to stay at school over Christmas! (The world famous Christmas Eve carol service is followed by a sung Eucharist on Christmas morning. The boys and their families then have lunch and their holidays begin in the afternoon.)

Finally, don't neglect those dusty old record cabinets which are well worth a pre-Christmas investigation. Gems can be unearthed here, such as *The Magnificent 700 – Music for Christmas.* This was recorded by BBC Radio Leeds on Abbey XMS 692 and contains the Leeds children's choirs and orchestra supplemented by the West Riding Singers, offering not only traditional carols but some beautiful lesser known ones such as 'Carol of the Huron Indians'.

Visits Despite all the disadvantages of December a well-planned visit in connection with Christmas offers a great deal of interest. This applies to schools located in either urban or rural environments.

Churches

One destination common to both is a local church. With very young children (and bearing in mind that many may never have been in a church) it is best to keep things simple. One way to do this is to pre-plan the visit along thematic lines which are all related to Christmas. Thus:

Light: churches are usually beautifully decorated at this time of the year and candles feature largely. Christmas trees are large and impressive and children are interested in stained glass windows – particularly if they have been working on these in their own classrooms.

Birth: pursuing this theme creates an opportunity to look at fonts. Whether these are Norman examples mounted on stone pillars, leaden as in twelfth century examples in Kent, or modern versions, they all stimulate children's interest when the rituals of baptism are described with them *in situ*.

Music: many vicars/curates are quite competent organists, and although this is a busy time of year for them, if they can meet the school party in church their expertise is invaluable. If they can be persuaded to play the organ this is a huge bonus, likewise if they can toll the bells and offer some comment about them. To expect the choir to be present is just about impossible but many choirs of bigger churches make recordings of their music these days. It might be possible when contacting the vicar or verger in advance to have a recording of the choir performing whilst the children are in the church.

Secrets: this is an imaginative theme for Christmas with young children, and again various aspects of a church can be incorporated into it. For instance an investigation for mason's marks always intrigues children. Likewise children are very excited to find the squints (sometimes known as hagioscopes), holes driven through the wall on either side of the chancel so that the high altar can be seen. A tour outside could also reveal gargoyles – another very popular discovery – and children enjoy seeing them in action as water spouts.

Journeys: outside the church the journey theme could be doubly pursued by the children's own 'journey' through the graveyard, and 'the journeys through life' as depicted on the various gravestones. Some very simple rubbings might be taken during this activity.

(Activity Sheet 28 relates particularly to church visits.)

Streets

Visiting familiar streets and markets can be an activity equally productive in town or village schools and again a thematic Christmas approach can help to focus on specific issues.

Decoration: How are the streets different from normal? What decorations can be seen in shop windows and in and on houses? How are these decorations different between day and night? Are there different noises coming out of shops and supermarkets? Are any special foods advertised in the shops? There is plenty of scope here for remembered observation which could result in good art/craft/technology work when the children return to school.

Presents: do the shops contain items which would make good presents? who for? How are they displayed? How do they try to catch your eye?

Communication: is the postman about more often? Are there more about? Are cards on display in shops? What wrappings are available in shops and post offices?

Weather: what is the weather like out on the street? is it 'Christmas weather' – what is 'Christmas weather'? Is there ice … what is ice? How are people dressed? Do you notice anything particular about cars or buses?

(Activity sheet 29 relates particularly to 'outside at Christmas' .)

The countryside

Once again, keeping it simple, a visit to the countryside in December can be very rewarding if it is well planned and prepared for. The theme throughout this outing can be 'detective work.'

The first exercise in 'spotting' might therefore be linked to birds. The most familiar winter bird to children is the robin, and if one is seen its aggressive chasing style can be drawn to the children's attention. Similarly if the location is right, an ivy covered wall, old shed etc., it might yield a robin's nest of woven grass, moss, dead leaves and a lining of feathers and hair.

Sparrows too are common and easily recognisable, as are starlings and blackbirds. With luck other birds which might be seen are jays, woodpigeons, great tits, chaffinches, yellowhammers and winter visiting lapwings.

If there is a covering of snow then the excitement of the detective work can be greatly increased by looking for bird's footprints. With children of this age, trying to differentiate between which bird's footprints are which seems too complex.

However such a covering of snow, and in the right environment, might lead to the discovery of animal tracks as well. Animals leaving their trails in these circumstances might include rabbits, field mice, squirrels, foxes, stoats and badgers.

There are several books to help with these activities and two of the best are: *Collins Guide to Animal Tracks and Signs* and the RSPB's *Bird Watcher's Pocket Guide*. The latter has the great advantage of living up to its description – it can be slipped into the shallowest of pockets!

It is worth maintaining the 'detective' theme for other aspects of a country outing too. Children like spotting holly bushes, particularly those splashed with the colour of red berries. Useful incidental information to give them here is that holly bushes can be very old – some being 300 years old – and their hard, heavy wood is no good for building purposes because it splits when dry.

'Spot the mistletoe' will get the children to look up, locating it in the branches of bare trees where it is a patch of green. Finally pine cone spotting might yield examples from such as spruce, Scots pine, larch, cedar and Douglas fir trees. Closer looks can sometimes show damage on the cones caused by squirrels in their search for food.

Places to visit

It is always worth checking local advertising to see what various museums, churches, cathedrals, theatres, castles, parks etc. are doing for Christmas. It is difficult to organise these into themes because of course their choice of material varies from year to year.

The details which follow indicate places/organisations who have put on Christmas presentations in recent years. For those within reach of various schools then a query via the telephone could lead to a good visit.

Museums
Geffrye Museum, Kingsland Road, London E2. (Tel. 0171 739 9893.) The staff of this museum are finely tuned to the needs of children and teachers. Not only have they had Wartime, Stuart and Victorian Christmas but they always manage to involve child visitors.

Bethnal Green Musuem of Childhood, Cambridge Heath Road, London E2. (Tel. 0171 980 2415.) This is another marvellous museum which presents everything with great discernment. There is usually a preview of their Christmas theme in November. It is always well worth a visit.

Museum of London, London Wall, EC2. (0171 600 3699.) One of the more recent offerings here was 'themed refreshments from different traditions'.

London Transport Museum, Covent Garden Piazza, WC2. (0171 379 6344.) Once again one of the highlights of this museum is the verve and enthusiasm of the staff with the children and their capacity to get their visitors involved.

Horniman Museum, Forest Hill, SE 23. (0171 699 1872.) Music and dancing from an Elizabethan Christmas was one of the features here, with authentic instruments such as viols, lutes and crumhorns.

Birmingham Museum and Art Gallery, Chamberlain Square (0121 235 2834)

Manchester Museum, Oxford Road, Manchester (0161 273 3333)

Chester, Grosvenor Museum, 27 Grosvenor St., Chester (01224 21616)

Newcastle-upon-Tyne, Joicey Museum, City Road (01632 324 562)

Oxford, Museum of Oxford, St. Aldates (01865 815 559)

Norwich, Castle Museum (01603 22233)

All six of these provincial museums have had Christmas themes in which children were actively involved.

Theatres
Barbican Centre, Silk Street, EC2 (0171 638 4141). The concourse often has interesting displays at this time of the year.

Royal Festival Hall, South Bank SE1 (0171 928 3191). As well as the performances inside the theatres there are often marvellous seasonal displays on the various levels, and live performances.

Other places
This list contains some very varied venues which are included because they have presented some special Christmas 'celebrations' in recent years.

Chiltern Open Air Museum, Newland Park, Gorelands Lane. Chalfont St Giles, Bucks. (01494 871117.)

'Fitzcarraldo', the theatre ship moored on the Manchester Ship Canal, Salford Wharf. (0161 873 7350.)

Carlisle Castle, Cumbria (01228 591922)

Prudhoe Castle, Northumberland (01661 833459)

Tredegar House, Newport, Gwent (1633 815880)

Tatton Park, Knutsford, Cheshire (01565 654822)

Dean Forest Railway, Norchard, Glos (01565 654822)

Nene Valley Railway, Wansford, Stibbington, Peterborough (01780 782854)

Syon Park, Brentford, Middlesex (0181 560 0881)

Visitors

Finally it is worth remembering how much pleasure visitors give to the children who are receiving them – and vice versa. This is the time of year to invite caretakers, cleaners, ancillary helpers, crossing patrols, members of nursing homes etc., to the classroom to share some of the joy of the season with their young hosts.

Non-human visitors should be catered for too – bird tables should be kept well stocked so that the children can enjoy seeing robins and other birds visiting their school.

Resources

Throughout this book resources have been recommended where it has seemed most appropriate. There are one or two other areas however where a little effort often reaps a great reward.

All Key Stage 1 teachers are aware of the value of trawling through colour magazines at this time of the year and many schools have stockpiles of cuttings from there from previous years. One of the findings which can stem from this source is a large, colour reproduction of a famous painting appropriate to Christmas.

Well displayed, these enhance the classroom and several are greatly enjoyed by young children. Examples which fulfil both these criterias are: 'Hunters in the Snow' by Breughel, 'Journey of the Magi' by Gozzoli, 'Head of a Clown' by Buffet, 'The Skaters' by Pieter Breughel the Younger, and 'Winter in Flanders' by Pieter Brueghel the Elder.

For those teachers who want to carry an art display further then it is always worth investigating loan services from education authorities, art galleries, museums.

Another source of smaller, but equally fascinating pictures at this time of the year is postage stamps. If some European ones can be obtained then this is a bonus. For instance in past years Czechoslovakian stamps featured 'Good King Wenceslas', 'Silent Night' featured on some Austrian stamps and a Hungarian series contained scenes for great fairy tales.

Finally, how do we find out what is new and good in children's books for Christmas? An invaluable magazine here is *Books for Keeps*. Subtitled the 'children's book magazine', and with reviewers who are frank and perceptive this is invaluable reading for all teachers. It can be obtained on subscription from: *Books for Keeps*, 6 Brightfield Road, Lee, London SE12 8QF. (Tel. 0181 852 4953.)

There are activity sheets associated with this chapter.

Sheet 28 is a sheet to use on a visit to a church. Children are asked to identify various features.

Sheet 29 requires the children to write something about the postman, illustrate some winter clothing and draw a robin. Holly has to be coloured in.

Party Time!

(Activity sheets 30 and 31)

Sad to say, in some instances, children's parties are now just replaced by a disco. This is a shame on several counts. Well-organised games based on a variety of activities are still hugely enjoyed by young children, and allow incidental learning to take place during their passage.

This chapter is in some ways an *aide-memoire*, for many of the games mentioned here are old favourites which have sometimes undeservedly been forgotten. Others are modified versions of games adapted for young children.

For ease of reference the activities have been arranged under five headings:

A Music and movement games.

B Moving games

C Searching games

D Sitting down games

E Noisy games

A Music and Movement Games

1 The farmer's in his dell

This is a very old favourite. The children join hands and form a large circle, leaving one of their number in the middle. He is 'the farmer'.

All then sing:

> 'The farmer's in his dell,
> The farmer's in his dell,
> Heigh ho the merry oh,
> The farmer's in his dell.'

The second verse replaces and repeats the first as follows:

> 'The farmer takes a wife'

During the singing of this the farmer chooses a wife to join him in the middle of the circle:

The game then continues:

> 'The wife takes a child...
> The child takes a nurse...
> The nurse takes a dog...
> The dog takes a cat...
> The cat takes a rat...
> The rat takes the cheese...'

Having then got a large group in the middle, the actions are reversed during the singing of:

> 'The farmer runs away...
> The wife runs away...'

This continues to the last verse of:

> *'The cheese stands alone,*
>
> *The cheese stands alone,*
>
> *Heigh-ho the merry oh,*
>
> *The cheese stands alone.'*

For those teachers who want to extend this game to involve some more extensive miming then the same tune can be used to incorporate different words and actions.

These could be:

> **'The farmer grows the wheat'** (mime showing how he prepares for this)
>
> *'The miller grinds the flour'* (grinding, filling the bags etc.)
>
> *'The baker makes the dough'* (appropriate mime)
>
> *'The grower sells the bread'* (appropriate mime)
>
> *'We all eat the slices'* (appropriate mime by all)

The scope for utilising this melody and idea is vitually limitless, and it could be extended to all sorts of occupations and activities.

2 The Hokey Cokey

Apart from being great fun this is a painless way of re-informing the children's awareness of right and left. Another advantage is that the music is very easy and can often be picked out in C by an average pianist without any recourse to written music.

The words are sufficient reminder of all the actions required:

> *'You put your right hand in*
>
> *You put your right hand out,*
>
> *You put your right hand in and you shake it all about,*
>
> *You do the Hokey Cokey and you turn around,*
>
> *That's what it's all about.'*

Chorus:

> *'Oh Hokey Cokey Cokey Cokey*
>
> *Oh Hokey Cokey Cokey Cokey*
>
> *Oh Hokey Cokey Cokey Cokey*
>
> *That's what it's all about.'*

The round continues

> *'Left hand…*
>
> *Right leg…*
>
> *Left leg…'*

Finishing with *'whole self in.'*

The latter offers a great opportunity for 'shaking all about' and the teacher can of course extend proceedings by any number of additions – left ear, right ear, left thumb, right cheek etc.

3 'When the music stops'

Pass the Parcel
There are several games in which 'when the music stops' is a key factor. Musical chairs is the most obvious, and still very enjoyable. 'Pass the parcel' is another. This can be enhanced by asking the person caught with the parcel to start unwrapping it with an unusual implement until the music starts again. Teachers will know their own children best here and of course safety arrangements are vital. However the unwrapping of parcels with forks, spoons etc. all adds to the fun.

Dressing-up race
Another possibility in this context is the dressing-up race. A pile of dressing-up clothes is presented to each group of children and then the music begins. When it is stopped the group which has 'dressed up' the most quickly and effectively is the winner.

The Dancing Broom
Finally there is the game which always seems to have overtones of the sorcerer's apprentice! Borrow a broom from the caretaker, select an 'odd one out' and arrange the rest of the children in pairs. Then, before the music starts, present the odd one out with the broom as his/her 'dancing partner'. This adds another dimension to the usual disco activity because when the music stops everyone has to change partners – and the odd one out must dance with the broom. Some marvellous improvisation usually accompanies this activity!

B Moving games

1 Follow the leader

Little needs to be said here except to emphasise variety. Not only can the leader go anywhere in the classroom but the raising of arms, skipping, sitting down, lying down etc. all adds to the enjoyable involvement.

2 Simon says

This could follow game 1 in quick succession and help to get the party going with a swing in its early stages.

3 Unusual relays

Clothes peg relay
Searching for some originality in the relay game format is a familiar exercise for teachers of young children. The example suggested here is fun, well suited to a party in that it requires little in the way of equipment, and good for enhancing the children's manipulative skills.

First of all stretch a clothes line across a far part of the classroom (or hall). Then divide the children into groups and give each group leader half a dozen clothes pegs. The game then begins with the leader pinning his clothes pegs on the line in front of his team. The second person has to take down the clothes pegs and bring them to the third team member who then puts them on the line again. The game then continues until every member of the team has had a turn.

Dressing-up relay
A second party-type relay is the one of where a case of dressing up clothes is put at the head of each team. This time the leader goes first, opens the case and dresses up in the contents. He/she then returns to the next person and disrobes. Number 2 person then dresses up, goes back to the case, disrobes and put the clothes back in the case ... and so on.

Fancy hats
The final relay suggestion is the 'fancy hats' race. A collection of different (and exotic if possible) hats can be made. One is then given to each group – making sure that all are of the same approximate difficulty to wear – and the relay proceeds as usual.

C Searching games

1 Find it

How green you are
Many searching games have arisen from the old Victorian parlour game of 'hunt the thimble', where one object was hidden. One development which can be played at a young children's party is 'How green you are'.

The seeker in this game is encouraged in his efforts by the rest of the class singing 'how green you are' at increasing volume as he gets nearer to the hidden object. Likewise the farther he gets away from it the more muted the singing.

This game has the advantage of all participating is some way but there is still the difficulty of a young child becoming frustrated if something cannot be found reasonably quickly. One way round this is to divide the class into groups. The teacher will have prepared the ground by hiding a large quantity of small objects round the room (beans, peas, marbles, buttons etc.) and the groups then have to find as many of these as they can in a given time. The group which unearths the most objects is the winner.

Hunt the alarm clock
Another group search of this nature – with the added attraction of a noisy finish – is the search for an alarm clock. Once again the class is divided into groups. Before the game starts the teacher hides an alarm clock which is set to go off in perhaps 10 minutes time. The groups begin the search and as soon as one person locates the clock he leaves it undisturbed but whispers his success to the rest of the group. They then sit down and enjoy watching the others looking round. When the alarm goes off all those who are still searching are out.

2 Spot it

A more subtle kind of searching game is the one which involves hidden movement. One version here involves gathering all the children together in a closely packed circle. The searcher stands in the middle of this circle.

A bean bag is then surreptitiously passed from one child to the next. The seacher doesn't know where it is starting from and each movement should be as covert as possible. If the searcher pounces correctly then the person caught with the bag takes position in the middle – and so it goes on.

3 Match it

This searching game requires a little more preparation by the teacher but in terms of excitement, and incidental manipulation skills, it is definitely worth it.

First of all as large a collection as possible of jars, bottles, plastic containers, and tins with screw tops should be made. Four boxes of these without their lids should be located in one area of the classroom, four boxes of the missing lids should be set up somewhere else. Obviously care should be taken to check that the respective boxes all yield lids which fit.

When this has been done the class could be divided into four groups and each group is directed to one box of containers and one box of lids. The game is then to see which group can match lids to containers the quickest.

D Sitting down games

I-spy

There is a time in all parties when the teacher wants activities to be fairly restrained – prior to, or immediately after tea is usually one such occasion! Sitting down games provide the opportunity to establish this sort of atmosphere.

The examples suggested here are in order of 'tranquillity' with the most ordered being first.

'I spy' needs no explanation but with young children sitting in a circle it is best if 'the little eye' sees only things in the classroom. The game can then progress gently for as long as the teacher wants it to.

Hot potato

With minimal equipment the circle can then move on to the next game. This is the almost equally well known 'hot potato'. A potato (or some similar object) is passed around until one of the children who is blindfolded shouts 'Hot!' The child holding the object at the time is then out and the game continues in the same way.

Remember

This game requires slightly more material and involves groups rather than individuals. This time a table of objects is located in the centre of the circle. There might be a dozen or more of these – pencil, ruler, doll, lunchbox, chalks, book etc. The children are divided into groups within the circle and the leader of each group (carefully chosen for obvious reasons!) is given a piece of paper on a clipboard, and a pencil.

The group are invited to look at the objects on the table for perhaps two minutes. Then a cloth is put over the table and the groups confer. The leader makes a note of each object remembered and the group with most, correct answers in the time limit is the winner. This game could be extended to include blindfold touching, smelling and listening to a collection of sounds.

Choose

The last game in this sub-section is a move on from 'Remember' in that all the children are now involved in a more tactile manner. Once again the teacher should make a collection of objects but as well as pencils, rulers, rubbers there should be smaller things such as buttons, screws, paper clips, small coins etc. The collection should be as large as possible and then subsequently divided into four piles.

The children are then divided into four groups, blindfold, and directed to sit round their particular collection of disparate objects. The object of the game is then to sort out the objects by feel alone. Associated skills come into play here for not only must the children recognise things by feel, but there is also the organisational aspect of what goes where, and how do we arrange it in a group when blindfolded.

The team which finally arrives with the best sorted piles is the winner.

E Noisy games

No party would be complete without noisy games, and they can be used as 'icebreakers' at the beginning, or for a finale before home time.

Who are you?
This is a good game to play when two classes are combining for a party – or a boys/girls competition where one class only is involved. The teacher should initially make a large collection of paper bags (under no circumstances should plastic bags ever be used).

Eye holes could be cut in these and at a chosen time the boys could be removed to put their bags over their heads, whilst the girls are doing the same somewhere else. (A similar situation will apply if two classes are involved.)

The groups are then brought together and the children guess 'who's who'. It adds to the fun if funny walks, disguised voices etc. are used.

What are you?
In this game the children are all secretly told that they are an animal – pig, horse, dog, cat etc. They are then told that there are, say, four animals the same as them in the room, and they have to find them.

At this point the children are told to make the noise of the animal they represent – thus dogs begin barking, pigs snorting, horses neighing etc.

Amidst the cacophony the children have to find the other 'animals' making the same noise as they are.

Stick it
For this game the teacher could do with an assistant to help blow up a considerable number of balloons! Once these have all been prepared the game is simple if vigorous!

The balloons are divided up into four groups of children and each group is given a wall of the classroom as 'their' area. The balloons are then rubbed as vigorously as possible on woollen clothing to generate sufficient static electricity to enable them to be stuck on the wall. This activity always involves a few explosions as well and the winning group is the one which gets most balloons sticking to their wall.

Activity sheet 30: Lucky number

There are two activity sheets associated with this chapter. Sheet 30 involves some simple adding of numbers for the children. The result of this addition gives them their 'lucky numbers' and all that goes with these.

Obviously the children will need teacher guidance in completing the card and it is most suited for those at the top of Key Stage 1. However it generates a great deal of fun (and learning!) and is well worth persevering with. To show things work out an excellent example could be taken as follows:

Name	L	E	R	O	Y		W	A	L	S	H
Numbers related	3	5	9	6	7		5	1	3	1	8
Add them up		3 + 5 + 9 + 6 + 7				+		5 + 1 + 3 + 1 + 8			

$$= 48$$

Add the two numbers of your answer until you only have one number left:

4 + 8 = 12

1 + 2 = 3

3 is your lucky number!

Once all the computations for the card are complete the children will then know their lucky numbers. The teacher could prepare a box of nine cards – numbered 1 – 9. Each card could then have some 'facts' of interest to the children written on them, e.g. if your lucky number is 3 your favourite colour is red; your favourite day is Thursday; your favourite season is winter; your favourite food is ice cream…

The teacher can make the 'lucky number' information as simple or as detailed or as varied as she wants – the children always enjoy it!

Sheet 31: Push to win

The possibilities for games with this card are considerable. Some suggestions are:

a The child lays the card with the bottom flush with the desk or table. They then use a counter, or cardboard cut out, about the size of a 50p piece. This is laid half on and half off the bottom of the desk and 'tapped' so that it fires up the card (as in shove-ha'penny). The number on which the counter is mostly resting is then written down. Subsequent 'goes' yield further numbers and each one is added to the total as the game progresses.

Thus playing individually the child can

i Count the number of turns it takes to reach 50 or 100 or whatever target the teacher selects.

ii get considerable adding practice *en route*.

b The game can be played in pairs or groups with the winner being the first one to reach the required total in the fewest goes.

c Another possibility for either individual or group use is to change the game to one of multiplication. This time the counter could have a number of one of the lower multiplication tables stuck to it. When it lands on a square then a multiplication rather than an adding exercise takes place.

d A further development of game c would be to have a little bag with varied numbered counters in it. These are selected at random without looking at them – thus varying the multiplication table on each go.

F Christmas Quiz

The final activity sheet for use with this book is Sheet 32, which is a Christmas Quiz.

A Christmas Quiz

Hi! What do you know about Christmas?

Can you write in the missing words?

| Mary | stable | bells | crackers | carols |
| Bethlehem | shepherd | star | candle | presents |

1 Jesus was born in a _____ .

2 The stable was in a town called _____ .

3 Jesus' mother was called _____ .

4 The three kings followed a _____ in the sky.

5 This is called a _____ .

6 We get _____ at Christmas.

7 These children are singing _____ .

8 This man looks after sheep.

He is called a _____ .

9 At Christmas we pull _____ .

10 At Christmas we hear _____ ringing.

On the other side of this paper draw:

a One of the three kings.

b A Christmas tree with decorations on it.

© 1998 Redvers Brandling/Nash Pollock Publishing

Sheet 1

❦ Tell Olek about Christmas ❦

This is Olek!
He comes from Mars.

He doesn't know anything about Christmas!

Can you answer his questions?

1 Olek: What did Mary ride on to Bethlehem?

Answer: _____

2 Olek: Who did the angels speak to in the fields?

Answer: _____

3 How did the Three Kings find Jesus?

Answer: _____

4 Olek: What was one of the presents the Three Kings brought? *Answer:* _____

5 Can you write down any of the clothes the shepherds wore? *Answer:* _____

6 What do you know about Bethlehem?

Answer: _____

7 Olek: What is the date of Christmas Day?

Answer: _____

Use the other side of this paper to draw a picture about Christmas. You can choose what it is.

Sheet 2

Christmas Patterns

Billy and Mandy are making Christmas decorations.

Can you finish their patterns?

Colour them in when you have finished.

Hi! I'm Billy

○ △ ▢ ▭ ○ △ ▭ ▭ ○ △

Hi! I'm Mandy

▭ ▭ ○ △ ▭ ▭ ○

Now make up two patterns of your own.

Now match these shapes with their names.

Use a different colour each time.

square

Circle

triangle

rectangle

Christmas Colours and Shapes

Here is Jessica and her Christmas tree.
Look for these shapes on the tree and
on Jessica's dress.

Now colour all

☆ yellow   ☐ red   ▭ blue   △ green   ○ brown

Now ...

How many ☆ are there? ...   How many ☐ are there? ...

How many ▭ are there? ...   How many △ are there? ...

How many ○ are there?

Can you write the names of
these shapes on the other
side of this paper?

Sheet 4

Your Christmas Diary

Sun	Mon	Tues	Wed	Thur	Fri	Sat
			1	2	3	4
5	6	7	8	9	10	11
12	13	14	15	16	17	18
19	20	21	22	23	24	25
26	27	28	29	30	31	

Last day of school – 17 December

Mummy's party – 18 December

I must post my letter to Father Christmas on 21 December

Mummy ices the Christmas cake on 23 December

We are going to a pantomime on 30 December!

Now answer these:

1 What day of the week is it when school ends?
   F _ _ _ _ _

2 What day of the week is Mummy's party?
   _ _ tur _ _ _

3 What day of the week must you post your letter to Father Christmas? _ u _ s _ _ y

4 What day of the weeks does Mummy ice the cake?
   _ h _ _ d _ _

5 What day of the week are we going to a pantomime? _____

6 What day of the week is Christmas Day?_____

7 How many days are there in December?_____

8 What is the day of the week, and date, of the last day of the month? _____

Shape quiz

Hi! Can you do my special Christmas maths quiz sheet?

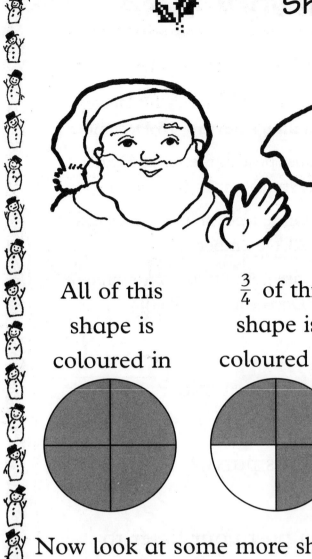

All of this shape is coloured in

$\frac{3}{4}$ of this shape is coloured in

$\frac{1}{2}$ of this shape is coloured in.

$\frac{1}{4}$ of this shape is coloured in.

Now look at some more shapes. Look under each one. It will tell you what to colour.

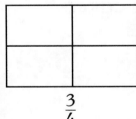

$\frac{3}{4}$

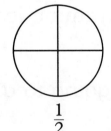

$\frac{1}{2}$

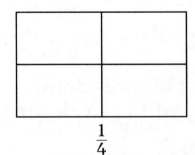

$\frac{1}{4}$

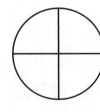

All

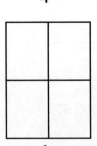

$\frac{1}{4}$

$\frac{3}{4}$

$\frac{1}{2}$

Sheet 6

Mandy's Christmas Day

Hi! I'm Mandy. This is what I did on Christmas Day.

1 What time did Mandy wake up?_____

2 What time was she going to church?_____

3 What was Mandy doing at 1.00?_____

4 What was Mandy doing at 3.00?_____

5 What time did Mandy go to bed?_____

Now, can you make up the story of your Christmas day?

On the other side of this sheet draw 5 clocks.

Put the time in them.

Draw pictures to show what you were doing at each time.

Sheet 7

🍂 Grandad buys his present 🍂

Hi! I'm Grandad Green I need your help!
I've got four grandchildren – Sharon,
Wendy, Shane and Mushtaq. Please help
me with the money for their presents.

Tent £6

Engine £4

Ball £2

Toy Soldier £1

Jigsaw £1

Doll £5

Book £3

Skipping rope £1

1 I buy Shane an engine. I buy Wendy a doll. What do I
   spend? _____

2 What do 2 toy soldiers cost? _____

3 Mushtaq wants a ball, a book and a jigsaw. What would
   that cost? _____

4 Sharon would like a doll, a tent and a skipping rope.
   What would that cost? _____

5 Which of these things costs the most? _____

6 How many toy soldiers could I buy for the cost of one
   engine? _____

7 Which three things cost the least? _____

8 What would these things cost all together? _____

Now turn over and draw three presents you would like.

Father Christmas's map

Ho! Ho! Help! Help! I can't find the way! Can you help me?

Supermarket

Ash Street

Jill

Lee

Park Road

Leroy

Low Street

Delia

Footpath

River

Park

1 Who lives in Park road? _____

2 Which street is Jill's house in? _____

3 What is the road next to the park? _____

4 Which road is nearest to the river? _____

5 Who lives in Low Street? _____

6 Who lives nearest the supermarket? _____

7 How does Leroy get to the supermarket? _____

8 How many houses are between Leroy's and Delia's?

_____

Favourite Carols and Colours

Look at this. It shows which Christmas carols some children liked best.

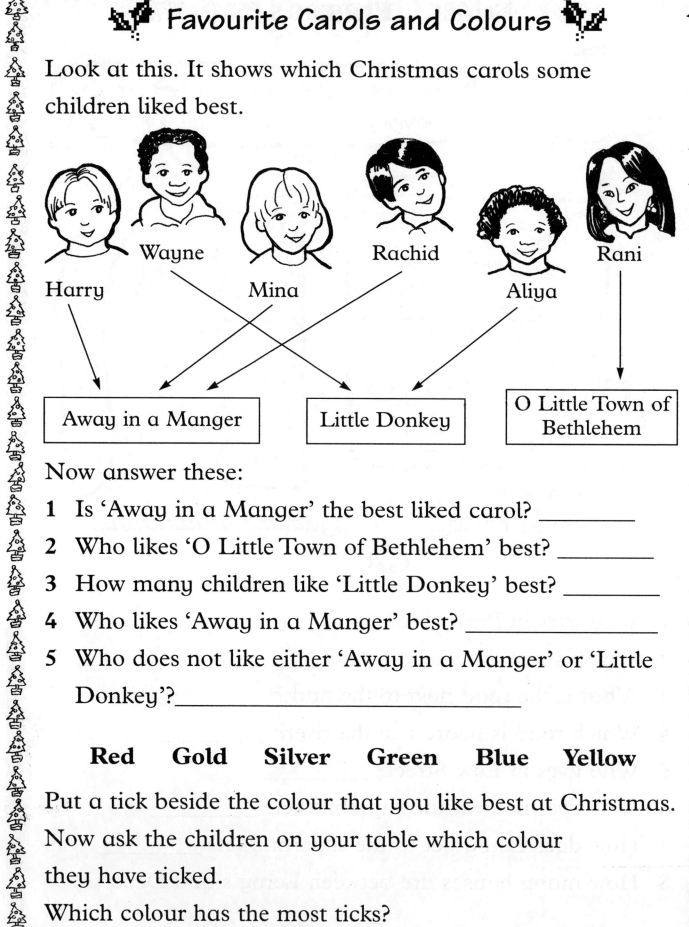

Now answer these:

1 Is 'Away in a Manger' the best liked carol? _____

2 Who likes 'O Little Town of Bethlehem' best? _____

3 How many children like 'Little Donkey' best? _____

4 Who likes 'Away in a Manger' best? _____

5 Who does not like either 'Away in a Manger' or 'Little Donkey'?_____

Red   Gold   Silver   Green   Blue   Yellow

Put a tick beside the colour that you like best at Christmas.

Now ask the children on your table which colour

they have ticked.

Which colour has the most ticks?

Presents

I took these presents to the Morley family. What can you tell me about them?

Mum

Daddy

Gran

Julie

Grandad

Paul

1 Who has the biggest present? _____

2 Who has the longest, thinnest present? _____

3 Whose present has got a triangle shape? _____

4 Who has the smallest present? _____

5 Whose present has an oval top? _____

6 If we took Julie's present away, how many would be left? _____

7 How long is Julie's present? _____

8 How many sides has Mum's present? _____

Now colour in all the parcels. Make them look like exciting presents.

❄ Number Quiz ❄

Can you do my number quiz?
Match the questions to the correct answer.
One is done for you.

$2 \times 5 =$

$\begin{array}{r} 10 \\ -7 \\ \hline \end{array}$

$\begin{array}{r} 8 \\ -8 \\ \hline \end{array}$

0

$4 \times 10 =$

3

10

How many 2s in 10?

5

3 – 6 – what comes next?

2 – 4 – 6 – 8 – 10 – what comes next?

12

$\begin{array}{r} 4 \\ 3 \\ 5 \\ +1 \\ \hline \end{array}$

9

3 – 6 – 9 – 12 – ? – 18
What number should be here?

13

40

1000
What is this
number called?

One thousand

15

Now … make up some of your own. Put them on the other
side of this paper. Can your friend get the answers?

Christmas Word Square

Can you find the Christmas words in here?

One is done for you.

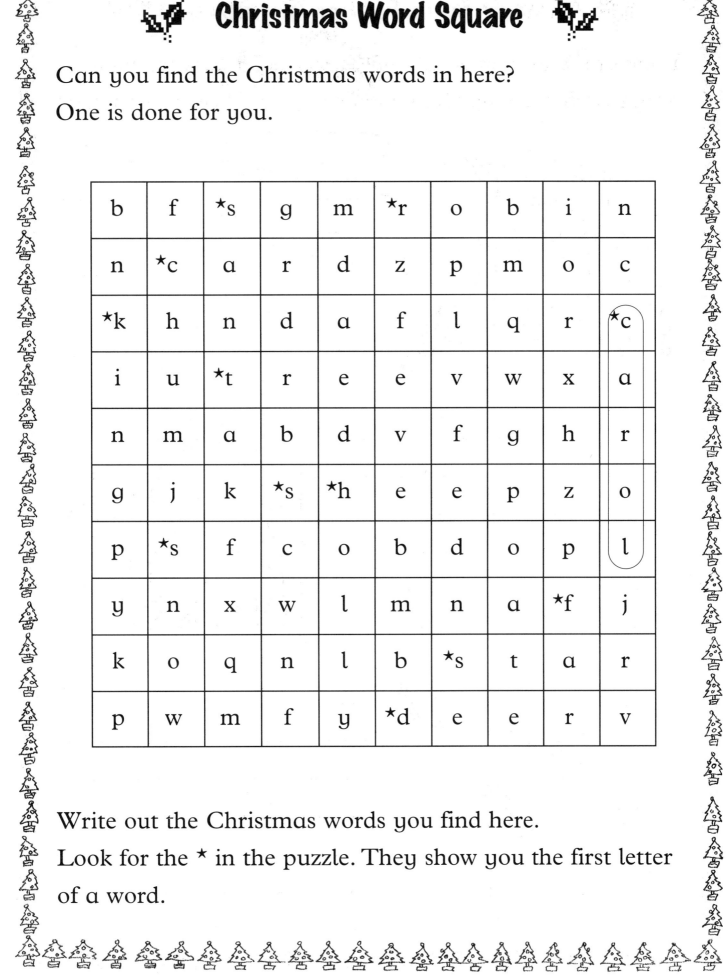

b	f	*s	g	m	*r	o	b	i	n
n	*c	a	r	d	z	p	m	o	c
*k	h	n	d	a	f	l	q	r	*c
i	u	*t	r	e	e	v	w	x	a
n	m	a	b	d	v	f	g	h	r
g	j	k	*s	*h	e	e	p	z	o
p	*s	f	c	o	b	d	o	p	l
y	n	x	w	l	m	n	a	*f	j
k	o	q	n	l	b	*s	t	a	r
p	w	m	f	y	*d	e	e	r	v

Write out the Christmas words you find here.

Look for the * in the puzzle. They show you the first letter of a word.

🍂 A letter from Father Christmas 🍂

Look at the drawings. Colour them in. Write something about each drawing (Remember Father Christmas's letter!)

Claus's Castle

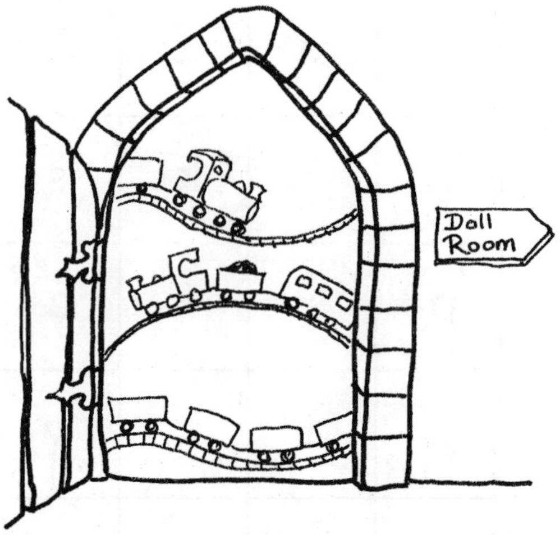

_____

_____

_____

_____

_____

_____

_____

_____

_____

_____

_____

Doll Room

_____

_____

_____

_____

_____

A letter from Ben

Hello. My name is Jacob. I had a letter from Ben. Can you answer these questions about his letter?

1 Where did Ben live? _____

2 Was the town crowded? _____

3 Who came to the door of Ben's Dad's inn? _____

4 What did the man at the door want?

_____

5 What did Ben have to do? _____

6 Who brought the baby presents?

_____

7 What was the baby's mother's name? _____

8 What did she say to Ben?

_____

On the other side of this paper draw a picture. Show Ben taking Joseph and Mary on the donkey, to the stable.

Sheet 15

Christmas Words

Here are some Christmas words.

They are mixed up.

Can you put them together again? Two are done for you.

Ca	ib	pres	ow
par	ar	sn	ent
tr	d	stock	ker
cr	rol	sa	ing
San	el	crac	erd
ki	ta	Jes	ck
hol	ing	Ma	ehem
car	ty	Bethl	ry
st	in	cand	us
rob	ee	sheph	le
ang	ly		

On the other side of this paper draw six of these things.

Then put their names beside them.

Mr Tibbs' Christmas Present

Here is a Christmas story. Can you put words in the spaces to make it a good story?

This is the story of a _____. His name was Mr Tibbs. On Christmas morning he walked into his _____. He saw lots of parcels beside the _____. Then he saw something else. It was a basket. There was something in the basket. It was another _____! 'But I am the cat in this _____!' said Mr Tibbs. Just then Jessica came over and picked Mr Tibbs up. 'You are still the cat in this house,' she said, 'But now you have got a friend to play with you.' Mr Tibbs wasn't very happy. Then he saw some _____ in his bowl. He bent down and drank the _____. Now he felt much better. He went to the _____. His friend was lying in it. 'Now,' said Mr _____. 'What shall I call you? I shall call you _____.' Jessica saw the two _____ looking at each other.

'I knew Mr Tibbs would like a _____ for Christmas,' she said.

Sheet 17

Christmas cards: the surprise package

A — A

Y - - - - - - - - - - - X

B - - - - - - - - - - - B

C - - - - - - - - - - - C

Y - - - - - - - - - - - X

D — D

King tag

Santa tag

Fold for sticking

The folding box

A

B

Tim's Christmas Present

Hi! You know who I am.

1 Write a title to suit this story. Then draw a picture for it.

Title _____

One Christmas Eve Father Christmas was riding through the sky. Suddenly one of his boots fell off!

It fell right down Tim Tubb's chimney. 'Father Christmas has been,' shouted Tim. 'I've got a present!'

'Oh dear,' thought Father Christmas. He looked round on his sledge. He saw Tim's present.

'Now,' he said, and dropped Tim's present after his boot.

'Whoosh!' The present landed in the boot just before Tim reached it.

'Wow,' said Tim. 'This must be a very special present. It came in a boot!'

2 Here is a title.

When Father Christmas came to my house.

On the back of this sheet write a story for it – and draw a picture.

Can you help Father Christmas?

Cut out the cards on this sheet.

Put them in a pack. Choose a card.

Tell the part of the story this card reminds you of.

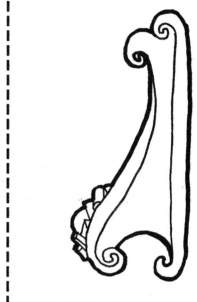

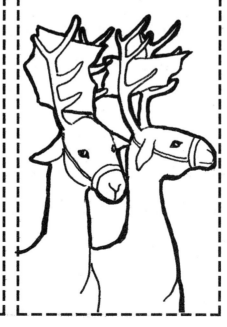
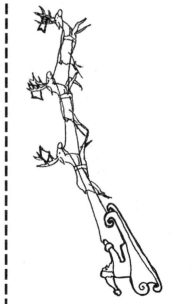

Now can you make some cards of your own which tell a story?

What are you doing for Christmas?

'Yes, Zerah had a great gift. But lots of people in our class have gifts too. Look…'

'We could share smiles. A smile makes everybody feel better. We could share energy. We could help our mums and dads and people who are older or not well.'

'We could share words. Words like 'please' and 'thank you' – and show we always mean them.'

'We could share being friends with other children who are not usually our special friends.'

'Dear God, This Christmas help us to share our gifts as much as we can. Help us to be kind and thoughtful, polite and helpful. Amen.'

 Christmas Peace

Winds through the olive trees
Softly did blow,
Round little Bethlehem
Long, long ago.

Sheep on the hillside lay
Whiter than snow;
Shepherds were watching them,
Long, long ago.

Then from the happy sky,
Angels bent low,
Singing their songs of joy,
Long, long ago.

For in a manger bed
Cradled we know,
Christ came to Bethlehem
Long, long ago.

Festivals!

Christmas   Divali   Hanukkah

These are all festivals.

Now choose a festival. Write down what you enjoy about it.

_____

_____

_____

_____

_____

Now draw a picture of something you have seen at this festival.

The mystery present

Who sent it?

Who is it to?

What is inside?

What happens when it is opened?

We get presents at festivals. Can you write a good story about this mystery present?

Sheet 26

🍁 The story of the carpet 🍁

Can you draw a picture for each piece of writing?

Guru Nanak sat under a tree in the village	Lots of people came to talk to him.
The carpet maker brought Guru Nanaka present. It was a carpet.	The carpet was put over the poor dog with the puppies.

Sheet 27

My church visit

The name of the church is: _____

1 What did you notice when you first came in?

_____

_____

2 What is the path leading to the altar called?

_____

3 Can you see a stained glass window? What colours are in it? _____

4 Is there a Christmas tree in the church? What is on the tree? _____

5 Can you find these things in the church?

A candle   **A cross**   **An organ**

A Bible   **A nativity scene**

Put a ✔ beside each one when you have found it.

6 Find a font in the church. When you have found it draw a picture of it here.

Find out what the font is used for. Write about this on the back of this paper.

Outside at Christmas

This man is very busy at Christmas.

Can you say who he is?

Write something about him here.

_____

_____

_____

What sort of clothes do we wear

on a cold day near Christmas?

Draw a picture of yourself in

your winter clothes.

Who am I?

I am a bird. I have a red breast.

I am cheerful. I sing at Christmas.

Answer: _____

Now draw me here.

What is the name of this tree?

_____ Colour it in.

On the other side of this paper draw a picture of a snowy

Christmas where you live.

Your lucky number

a	b	c	d	e	f	g	h	i	j	k	l	m	n	o	p
1	2	3	4	5	6	7	8	9	1	2	3	4	5	6	7

q	r	s	t	u	v	w	x	y	z
8	9	1	2	3	4	5	6	7	8

Write your name here: _____

Write the numbers
under each letter of   _____
your name here:

Add up all the numbers: _____

Add the two numerals of your answer together until you
only have one number left: _____

This is your lucky number!
Put it in here!

Sheet 30

Push to win

1	2	3
4	5	6
7	8	9
10	11	12

Go and win!

Sheet 31

Name . . . .   Date . . . .

❧ Christmas Quiz ❧

1 How many kings were there? _____

2 What colour are holly berries? _____

3 Put in the missing letters: m _ nc _   p _ es

4 How did the kings find their way to Bethlehem?

   _____

   _____

5 Put these letters in the right order:

   r a c e r c k

   Now draw what it is.

6 Finish the first line of this carol:

   Away in a _ _ _ _ _ _ .

7 Here is a riddle:

   We hang it up on Christmas Eve.

   It can be made of wool.

   If we are lucky we get presents in it.

   What is it? Draw a picture of one here.

8 What is this animal?

   Why was it important

   at the first Christmas?

   _____

   _____